EXTRAORDINARY ORDINARY WOMEN
~ OF NORTH WILTSHIRE

For Nick and Verity, with all my love

Illustrated by Lucia Lovatt **https://www.paintingsbylucia.co.uk/**

Extraordinary Ordinary *Women*

~ *of North Wiltshire*

Lucy Whitfield

THE HOBNOB PRESS

First published in the United Kingdom in 2024

by The Hobnob Press,
8 Lock Warehouse, Severn Road, Gloucester GL1 2GA
www.hobnobpress.co.uk

British Library Cataloguing in Publication Data
A catalogue record for this book is available from the British Library

ISBN 978-1-914407-66-6

Typeset in Chaparral Pro, 11/14 pt
Typesetting and origination by John Chandler

Contents

Acknowledgements

THANKS FOR SUPPORT, energy and enthusiasm go to Louise and John of Hobnob, for their unstinting work and help in putting this book together, and to Lucia for wonderful artwork, coaching, caffeine and mentoring. To Sarah for her lovely song and getting what I've been banging on about for years. To Liz for letting me loose on researching her maternal family and inadvertently providing the spark to found my women's history project. To Helen, Dan and Jenny for endless cheerleading, sound-boarding, hugs, and a wonderful musical backdrop. To Laura and Bettina for caffeine, beer and snarky feminist conversations. To Chris and Fi, Andy, Malc and Lou for being a fab cheering squad. To Elaine, Melissa and all the team (past and present) at Chippenham Museum, Julie and all the wonderful staff at Wiltshire and Swindon History Centre who've aided many of my discoveries, and Tracy, Charlotte and the team at Chippenham Library for providing support and a nurturing space. To Cina and Mike at Cousin Normans for incredible coffee and a warm and welcoming work space; Linds at the Old Road Tavern for giving me great cider and an extension to my living room; Steve and Linda, formerly of the Three Crowns, for encouragement, ale and an amazing platform to work from. To the people of North Wiltshire, and Chippenham in particular, for absorbing me, entrancing me, and letting me tell the stories of your town. To people who've taken the time to tell me about their granny – particularly Philip and Carole Yeates, and Lucy Scott-Ashe. To everyone who has believed that their female relative could be more than just that. Lastly, and most importantly, immense thanks and love go to my immediate family: Lin, Rob, Will, Sarah, Kate, Graham, Drew, Mary, Mike, Neil, Jilly, Liz, Huw and Simon for their love, support and suggestions, being sounding boards, help with the business and research, and fostering a deep love of history and caring for people from all walks of life. And finally, to my partner Nick and daughter Verity for their love and unwavering support for the career I'm making for myself.

Lucy Whitfield

Mary Unknown

You're a gap in the pages of history
You are one of the names left unsaid
You're one of the many, a mystery
where the records don't speak of the dead.

And did he call you his sweetheart
His dearest, his darling, his own
But he never wrote down your story
Mary Unknown

Your mother, your sister, your daughter
You lived all the life was your lot
Housework and children and water
Your toils and your triumphs forgot

All the meals served up from your kitchen
Made from the garden you'd grown
They didn't count for your story
Mary Unknown

You are nowhere in the records
There's space for the husband, not wife
No room for your triumph or awards
No matter how hard fought your life

What did you do with your daytimes
When all the children were grown
They didn't care for your story
Mary Unknown

Your granny, your aunt and your cousin
Passed over by government men
While men's names writ down by the dozen
And your name's forgotten again

All the stitches you made in the evenings
Sat by the fire alone
They never tell of your story
Mary Unknown

You're a great, broken gap in our story
Your troubles, discoveries, pride
Your wisdom, your tragedy, glory
Forgotten and hard cast aside

We'll sing your name to the people
So you'll be once again known
We'll tell the truth of your story
Mary Unknown
We'll tell the truth of your story
Mary Unknown

Sarah Callaghan

'History has failed to see women as workers, to see beyond their traditional roles to their hands and their brains, and so the memory of their achievements has been lost, again and again.
And so, again and again, women have to reinvent the wheel, being seen as possessing equal potential to men. Maybe a woman invented the actual wheel. We'll never know.'

Ailsa Holland,
About Time: Putting Women Back Into History,
TedX talk in Macclesfield, 2019

'But where's Florence Hancock?'

I ALWAYS SAY that I collect interesting women, both personally and professionally.

And if I'm out working, for example selling books at a craft fair or talking to a community group, I often speak to people who express their disappointment that I haven't included women like Chippenham's unioniser Dame Florence Hancock, Corsham and Kington Langley's author Heather Tanner, Swindon's suffragist Edith New, and Wilton's writer and socialite Edith Olivier in my work on Wiltshire women. They're not in this book either, fine and inspiring though their stories are.

My reply is always that they know who these women are already, to be able to ask me about them, and that's fabulous. And why not find out about someone new?

The chances are that these are the only names that come to people's minds because of a reliance on tokenism in women's history. Author Ailsa Holland argues, and I agree, that we're so conditioned to women's lives and achievements being marginalised in the historical narrative that we think that once we've found one exception, we don't need to look for any more women. And we – however unconsciously – use these women as a bit of an excuse to forget all the others or not bother to seek them out.

So, if asked to name a woman scientist, rather than just a scientist, nine out of ten people would probably say Marie Curie. Rather than Rosalind Franklin, Gertrude Elion, Barbara McClintock, Elizabeth Garrett Anderson, Elsie Widdowson, and so on. Similarly, a historic woman author request would probably result in a Bronte sister or Jane Austen, rather than L. T. Meade, Virginia Woolf, George Eliot, Kate Greenaway, Mary Shelley, Sarah Josepha Hale, etc. And the awesome achievements of suffragists are never too far away from these conversations either.

The rash of publications that seek to popularise women's history, particularly in the wake of the 100th year anniversaries of universal suffrage in the UK and USA, probably don't help this phenomenon either. They will regurgitate the same women again and again, adding in a smattering of others from the STEM field or sport, but generally contributing to the sense of malaise that these are the only women of history worth knowing about. They are a great starting point, but rarely do they encourage people to look beyond.

One of my biggest aims in my work in women's history is to sidestep any tokenism, and to seek out women from the available records that haven't come into the spotlight before, for whatever reason.

None of the women in this collection were widely known about before I dug into them, but some might have been mentioned in passing. All were found in the public domain – census records, birth marriage and death records, medical texts, case books, registers, travel records, church records, books of photos, old newspapers, maps, museums, Google. Oral history from relatives, some of whom I've tracked down, is the icing on the cake. The process is about following a story through, and not accepting that how someone is presented to us through available records - invariably merely listed as a wife or daughter of someone – doesn't mean that she didn't have an interesting life or wasn't valuable.

By this method, my women's history project – *The Women Who Made Me* – has covered a huge spectrum of women's history. The project has profiled nuns, penitents, criminals, divorcees, weavers, landladies, social pariahs, farmer's wives, cooks, women's officers, prodigies, suffragists, anti-suffragists, travellers, hawkers, prostitutes, social workers, gentry, workhouse inmates, engineers, stockbrokers, mothers of fourteen, mothers of none, mothers of illegitimate children, artists, musicians, manageresses, letter carriers, writers, performers, mathematicians, prison wardens, matrons, highwaywomen, confectioners, travellers, teachers, ballet dancers, factory workers, and someone who recommended do-it-yourself enemas. These are all important and diverse parts of women's history, but not all of them from Wiltshire, which is why you'll only find a selection of these in this book.

When I mention that I'm a women's historian, I usually get one of two reactions.

Firstly, someone will say 'Oh, I love the suffragettes!', because in many people's brains – particularly given the way history has been taught in school until relatively recently – women's history equals suffrage and nothing else. Perhaps they'll have touched on women's liberation matters too, and mention a burning bra, but invariably it's the Pankhursts and sometimes Millicent Fawcett that get the headlines. To that end, I've included a couple of Wiltshire suffragists in this collection, as they're worthy of note, but they're not front and centre or ahead of any other women in the book.

The second reaction I receive is to be told that 'my granny was a really strong woman'. Sometimes it's their great grandmother or maiden aunt, but almost never their mother (perhaps we're too close to our mothers temporally to see their achievements as significant). I've always found that statement fairly problematic, particularly as it implies that their Strong Granny was an exception and that most other women of that time were weak and not worth looking at – and on the evidence presented within these pages we can see that that really wasn't the case.

The other problem is that when I ask what Strong Granny did, the usual answer is 'well, she wasn't a suffragette or anything, but she worked so hard and faced so many problems', so we're back to only valuing women if they're involved in suffrage. Again.

The crux of this is that we have to stop looking at women for what they were not, and instead start finding value in who they actually were. Begin reframing what we do have in our women's ancestry and our historical society rather than decrying what we might feel is an omission due to what we've been taught to value.

Part of that means changing the way we look at how the history of ordinary people is presented to us. Many original historical records were written by and for those in administrative-style jobs at that time – for example, most census enumerators were men, at least in the 19th century, and they were collecting information for other men. Working women, even if they were literate, were more likely to be involved in the manual side of paid work rather than collecting data or writing for different purposes.

Most married women had a blank box beside them on census returns, because the gaze that was collecting that information didn't consider their day-to-day lives of interest or even worth recording. And I feel that to be a true women's historian, that gaze has to be challenged and not perpetuated.

Who said that a woman who gave birth eleven times, brought up eight of those children, and kept a house clean without chemical cleaners or a vacuum didn't have value? Just because it was the norm back then, doesn't mean that it wasn't an achievement. And was a woman on a farm, or in a shop or a pub really doing nothing – or was she working equally hard but her husband is being credited with her achievements due to laws around property?

In my talks, we do an exercise on Filling the Blank Box – where we look at what actually fills that married woman's blank occupation box on the census. I throw props around the room – a handful of dolls to represent multiple children, a washboard for the physical work of the laundry, a box of yeast for baking and brewing, a scrubbing brush for endless cleaning, a saucepan for food preparation, toy animals for livestock care, dressmaking scissors for clothes making, a darning mushroom and ball of yarn for clothes maintenance, a bandage for family illness care, a gardening fork for growing food, a spindle and fleece for spinning, and so on. I'll also add in a few things that might not have been recorded either – an accounts ledger for the women who did the books for the business that was technically her husband's, a pair of flying goggles for aeronautical engineers who would have been seen as hobbyists, a beer tankard for women who ran a pub while her husband had another job but he had to hold the licence.

At the end of this, we have an enormous pile of props that all relate to women's daily lives, and fill that blank box to bursting. Showing that married women didn't really have nothing to show for their lives back then, but more that it was perceived that way by people who didn't understand or value that life. The trick is to remember that pile when faced with a woman's records, and not take what's written (or not) about them at face value.

At the other end of that scale, societally we were taught to pity unmarried women, because they haven't fulfilled their 'womanly potential' – or 'getting married and raising a family', as it's known. Thankfully we've now mostly moved on from that view, but in oral history the view that spinsters were unlucky and had somehow had the bum deal has been passed down to us by people who did 'fulfil their potential', because otherwise we wouldn't be here. And often it's the unmarried women who had the freedom to explore more of life.

It's about listening hard to the way history has been presented to us, and questioning the language and statements used. Women who achieved despite male-dominated society and broke glass ceilings are often talked about via parameters that would be applied to men of that time, and we should perhaps rather be about expanding value of the full female life experience – Ginger Rogers having done all the dancing too, but backwards and in high heels, so to speak. Or, in many cases, in spite of societal obstacles and with a clutch of children at your skirts.

So, against this background, I present to you twenty case studies of extraordinary ordinary women drawn from North Wiltshire – from Malmesbury in the north of the county, to Winterbourne Bassett in the east and Corsham in the west. And as far south as Bradford on Avon and Devizes. Many of them are from my adopted home of Chippenham.

At a first glance, many are names that aren't instantly recognisable, though if you know the county you'll find familiarities in spaces and places that are woven into their tales. There are early Mormons, three gentry sisters, an 18th century chemist/druggist, two women who struggled with mental health issues, two social workers – one also an artist, one also a writer, teachers, a World War Two heroine, and many more besides. Some were wives and mothers, others not.

Enjoy getting to know these people, and becoming familiar with them until their names roll off your tongue as easily as Marie Curie, Charlotte Bronte and the Pankhursts, or even Florence Hancock or Heather Tanner. Then move on and seek out more interesting women and their stories – they're out there.

Cassia Denne

F OR MUCH OF the 20th century, school head teachers were supposed to be formidable and particularly scary, so a visit to them or even just an interaction should have put the fear of God into a pupil. However, Miss (Edith) Cassia Denne, who was the first head of Chippenham's Girls High School in 1956, still has a reputation among women of the town for being particularly fierce and terrifying. The school buildings have now been incorporated into the town's Hardenhuish School, but the girls' school she founded fully came to an end in 1976.

Like any scary teacher though, Cassia was in fact only human – although that fact often does not occur to pupils – and had a life before and outside the school she presided over. She gained a science degree at a time when women attending university was still very rare, and science was still considered mostly a boy's subject. She even at one point joined a convent. And, quite reasonably, had taught at various other schools before appearing in Chippenham.

Edith Cassia was the first child of her father's second family, born in 1906 in a village just outside Canterbury. She was followed four years later by her brother William. Her father had previously been married to a woman named Harriet, and Cassia and William had older half-siblings – Esther, Amelia and Percy – who appeared not to live with them while growing up by virtue of being much older. Harriet had died in 1903, and Cassia's father (a bricklayer employed by Canterbury cathedral) married her mother Emma in 1905. Both were from Kent, born and bred.

Cassia was educated at Simon Langton Girls Grammar School in Canterbury, being bright enough to pass the entrance requirements and rise to the top of the school. This school still exists, although the buildings she would have attended were destroyed in the Second World War. Her father died in 1917, when he was 60 and Cassia was around 11, and as such would have been too old to fight in the First World War. Her mother then took in boarders from the local Canterbury barracks to make ends meet.

Cassia, once she had finished school, then went on to the University of London, and gained a BSc in the sciences in the early 1920s. She took her mother with her to help her out with domestic duties while she was studying. Bringing along mum was quite common for single women at this time as they were embarking on a career.

Chippenham Girls High School appeared not to keep a record of their staff's careers before joining the school – this was often more common to long-established grammar schools – so Cassia's full career before she arrived in Chippenham is a little hazy. However, a *Bury Free Press* newspaper article reporting her headship of a previous school has given some clues to where she taught and lived.

She began her teaching career in 1928 after completing her degree. Going in to teaching was often the choice of bright young women coming out of university at this time, as it enabled learning to continue and gave the chance to impart what you'd learned so far to young minds. A degree was not required to become a teacher, particularly for women, but it did mark out women as committed and ambitious. There was also a marriage bar for female teachers at this time, meaning that if Cassia had married she would have not been able to keep her job. However, that does not have been a consideration for Cassia. This bar was removed for the London school boards in 1935, but not for the rest of the country until 1944.

She initially taught at Blackburn High School, in Lancashire, and by the late 1930s Cassia was on the staff of Dame Alice Owen's School in Islington. She was living with her mother Emma in Hendon for much of that decade, so it's possible that she moved to Dame Alice Owen's quite quickly. By 1939 she was established as very much a part of Dame Alice Owen's as the biology mistress.

At the outset of the Second World War in the autumn of 1939, the school moved as one to Kettering in Northamptonshire, taking all the teachers and evacuating the students. Cassia initially lived in

Kettering, in digs alongside the school secretary Rita Shead. Her mother went to Harpenden in Hertfordshire instead, so they were separated, at least initially. About a year later the boys' part of the school moved to Bedford, where it remained for the rest of the war, but the girls stayed in Kettering – alongside various other evacuated schools from London, including St Aloysius' Convent School, two Catholic primary schools and Clark's Secretarial College.

One of her pupils, Veronica Pinckard, remembered an incident involving Cassia during these years:

> On our way to school one lovely, hot sunny day, my friends and I were enjoying an ice-cream cone when we spotted Miss Denne, our biology mistress. They threw theirs in the gutter, but I was a thrifty little soul and hated waste. Putting it in my pocket was a messy idea and hiding it behind my back seemed childish, so I brazened it out. Miss Denne was furious. 'Eating in the street – in uniform – without gloves, Veronica is very low class. You shall not make a mockery of Dame Alice Owen's. You will report to the headmistress immediately.' She confiscated my blazer and straw hat, which was pointless as I was wearing the very distinctive saxe blue dress with the school emblem emblazoned on the breast pocket. Everyone in town knew which school we belonged to.
>
> Miss Bozman, the headmistress, scolded me rather gently, told me to be more circumspect, reminded me to wear gloves at all times and not to eat ice cream in public. It was unladylike, and I must always uphold the traditions of our illustrious school. Then with my promise to do just that, she gave me back my blazer and hat.

Veronica, perhaps understandably given this incident, had no love for Cassia, describing her as 'mean', and as someone who delighted in dissecting insects and frogs as part of her biology lessons.

This episode shows the respect for ladylike qualities, and class boundaries, that were expected of young women at the time, and that had been bred and enforced into women like Cassia. Teachers considered it their job to enforce these morals into their charges, and were rarely off duty. Eating in the street was seen as vulgar, and uncouth, much as being improperly dressed without a hat and gloves, and was part of a peculiarly British sense of morals, and all about outward appearances.

The original Dame Alice Owen's School girls' buildings were bombed in 1940, so the school did not return until 1945. Cassia went back to London with them, and her classrooms were now temporary huts on the former school site. She rose to become their senior science mistress, and lived in Finsbury with her friend school secretary Rita. Whether Rita was anything more than a friend is open to question. Unmarried female teachers often lived together in pairs, outwardly for support and companionship. Any romantic nature to this partnership would not have been remarked upon publicly, but it is always possible that her friendship with Rita had greater depth.

In 1950, fancying a change, Cassia took on her first school headship. She moved to become the third headmistress of the girls' part of the Silver Jubilee Schools in Bury St Edmund's, Suffolk. The schools, established in 1935 to commemorate the 25th anniversary of George V having the British throne, had at this stage evolved to be part of the Secondary Modern schools that had been created in the tripartite system in 1944, providing a general extended secondary education and training for pupils not expected to go on to higher education. In the early days of these schools, the provision was continuing the elementary school style education that had flourished since the 19th century, but gradually more ideas were added to the curriculum and in some towns the main employers would have an influence on the skills the children learnt.

Here, under Cassia's jurisdiction, the sexes were kept strictly separate at the school, with a white dividing line in the playground. In addition to further English, Maths, Science, Scripture and some humanities subjects, the girls studied commercial, secretarial and nursing courses. Domestic science, often the backbone of girls' education at the time, was also heavy in the curriculum, which would have encompassed food technology and techniques, textiles, and other home economics skills.

Four years later, having been well respected in the town as the head mistress of the school, Cassia decided on a full career change. She left the world of schools behind, resigning her head teacher position, and planned to enter a convent.

At this stage, in 1954, she was 48 and at the top of her profession – and may have felt that the life of a nun was right for her in terms of both spiritual and career fulfilment. She would also have long gone past the age where most women of the time expected to marry, should she have been that way inclined, even though she could now do so and keep her job. Or this may have been a long-cherished ambition for her. Whatever her reasoning, she handed over her Bury St Edmunds school to the next head teacher Edith Crocker, and prepared to take holy orders.

Exactly what happened next is not known, but Cassia did not last more than two years in the convent. Whether it was that being a nun was not what she expected it to be, or she missed teaching too much, she returned to teaching in 1956. She took on the position of head teacher at the brand-new girl's high school – another secondary modern establishment – in Chippenham, a market town in Wiltshire. Her friend Rita seems to have moved with her to the town.

Chippenham Girls High School was opened 10 September 1956, by education secretary and Chippenham MP Sir David Eccles and his wife Sybil, taking the girls away from the mixed secondary modern which had operated out of the old grammar school site on Cocklebury Road since the Chippenham Temporary Senior School was formed in November 1940.

The new building was close to the buildings that the grammar school had moved to in 1939, and had been purpose-built for their use. Four years of schooling were offered at the time, from 11 until the school leaving age, which was then around 14, so at the end of what was is now called Year 10. There were 486 girls on the roll at the beginning of the school, with 22 teaching staff and a school secretary. They offered English, maths, science, music, history, and a lot of domestic science. With a nod towards the surrounding area, the school also offered rural subjects.

They supported some girls who had already started work towards their General Certificate of Education (GCE) – but the ambition of Cassia and her school was to further improve the depth of the education offered to the girls of the town. The staff wanted to aim for the University of Cambridge courses, not the Associated Board syllabus that they had been working to before, and one of the first subjects discussed at staff meetings was the provision of advanced courses (beyond the GCE examinations) in Secondary Modern Schools.

This came to fruition quickly – two years after the school's founding, in 1958, there were over 600 girls on the roll, and the school offered a Fifth Form and even had a lower Sixth Form. And by 1959 there was a full opportunity for girls to study either for GCE, general subjects, or practical courses, and they were streamed accordingly. Shortly after this, commercial subjects were added to the senior school provision.

In terms of school life, Cassia's school log book regularly records sports matches against other local secondary modern schools – those in Melksham, Malmesbury and Calne most often – and athletics tournaments, with educational trips and visits from speakers intended to inspire the pupils.

For example, a representative of Simplicity Dress Patterns (clothes making was an important skill when very little came ready-made) visited in October 1958, and the school held a fashion show to demonstrate the skills they'd learned, and in 1966 they hosted Flying Officer PL Sturgess of the WRAF to talk to the girls about opportunities in the armed forces. And in July 1959 the BBC radio discussion programme 'It's My Opinion' was broadcast from the school hall.

Some pupils remember that when the neighbouring boys' school opened across the field at what is today Sheldon School, Cassia altered the start and finish times of the school to discourage her girls from spending time with the boys on the way to and from school.

Cassia remained at the school until the summer of 1966, having presided over some initial discussions about integrating secondary education in the town a couple of years earlier, although this did not take place for several more years. She'd had a period of ill health just after Christmas in 1966, and had lost her mother the previous year, so at the age of 60 took retirement. There was a presentation made for her in that July, with guests served tea in the library afterwards. At retirement, she was a member of the South Western examinations board for the certificate of Secondary Education.

She returned to the school at least once more, to talk about its history at a celebration event in 1975, alongside the school's second head teacher Miss Wilkins.

At this stage she was living with her dear friend Wendy, and they moved to a bungalow overlooking Bath, where she reputedly offered tutoring to some select children. Her former friend Rita remained in Chippenham, so Cassia's living arrangements had moved on.

Cassia and Wendy then spent her last years together by the sea, on the south coast of England at Worthing in Sussex. She died there in 1991, aged 85, and is buried at Durrington Cemetery. Her death notice in the Bury Free Press notes that she was dearly loved by Wendy and her many friends.

References

Adams, C (1982), *Ordinary Lives*, Virago Press
Bristol Evening Post, 17 December 1965, *'Girls' Head is to retire'*
Bury Free Press, 5 May 1950, *'New School Head Here'*.
Bury Free Press, 30 July 1954, *'From one head to another'*

Bury Free Press, 13 September 1991, *'Deaths'*

England and Wales: Birth, Marriage and Death Records, held by Ancestry.co.uk

Jefferies, S (1987), *A Chippenham Collection*, Chippenham Civic Society

Hardenhuish School Log Books (held at Wiltshire and Swindon History Centre)

Hardenhuish school records, various, held by Wiltshire and Swindon History Centre

Hazells Histories, *Lost Bury St Edmunds*: https://www.hazells.co.uk/2020/09/03/lost-bury-st-edmunds/

Pinckard, V (2012), *A Damn Fine Growth: Autobiography of a Cockney Kid*, Xlibris US

UK 1901 census, held by Ancestry.co.uk

UK 1911 census, held by Ancestry.co.uk

UK 1939 register, held by Ancestry.co.uk

Western Daily Press, 13 May 1963, *'Growing up is Lesson No 1'*

Wiltshire Times and Trowbridge Advertiser, 15 September 1956, *'New School For Girls'*

Wiltshire Times and Trowbridge Advertiser, 29 September 1956, *'Photograph and caption of Chippenham Girls' High School Staff'*

Wiltshire Times and Trowbridge Advertiser, 6 October 1956, *'Sir David enjoys his job! Opens new girls' school at Chippenham'*

Mary Harding or Pepler or Hancock

I T IS A bit of a myth that married women didn't work in Victorian times – they often did, whether it was acknowledged or not. Unacknowledged roles might be serving behind the bar in the family pub, having their own jobs on a farm, or doing the accounts for her husband's business. All these women would still leave the profession box blank on a census return – the job was their husband's, and therefore the work was attributed to him.

When it came to acknowledged work, low pay on behalf of their husbands would often mean that married women had to juggle childcare alongside a job, whether it was taking in laundry to make ends meet, or having a more formal role in a factory. However, respectable married women were not supposed to work in polite society – but if you had faced stigma from various different sources all your life, this probably mattered less as to how you saw your place in the community, and you carried on regardless. And this work ethic could help inspire those who came after you.

Mary Pepler/Hancock, née Harding, was a married worker, with 14 children under her belt by the time she'd reached her 40s, and continually worked as a cloth weaver throughout her life. But she probably had faced enough stigma through her earlier life that any censure for working was water off a duck's back.

The fact that she was a cloth weaver came from her parentage. Her father William Harding had worked as a cloth weaver himself since his early teens, and many of his nearest and dearest worked throughout their lives too, whether they were male or female.

Mary was born in December 1859 at Rhydyfelin, South Wales – in modern day Rhondda Cynon Taff, not far from Pontypridd. The cloth industry of the late 1850s, in that area, was small. There was one mill, at Upper Boat and Rhydyfelin on the banks of the river Rhondda, which was run by Evan and James James. This had a small workforce, of which Mary's father William, and possibly her mother Fanny, was part. Evan and James James, though cloth factory owners, are better known as the composers of *Hen Wlad Fy Nhadau* or *Land of My Fathers*, the Welsh National Anthem, and a statue commemorates them in Pontypridd.

Fanny was William's third wife. Mary had a living brother from his first marriage, no siblings from his second, and then an older brother – Edward – from his marriage to Fanny. They were joined by sisters – Frances and Sarah, who lived, and Ann, who didn't. Though William came from Wiltshire and Fanny from Somerset, the family moved around a great deal, going where the work was. They spent time around Bradford on Avon, Trowbridge, Tiverton and Chard in Somerset, and Cam and Wotton Under Edge in Gloucestershire, but Mary was the only child born in Wales.

Fanny died in 1869, when Mary was around 10, and her father very quickly married a fourth time – to Caroline. Mary gained a step-brother near her own age, and later on four more siblings, all but one of whom who lived.

On the face of it, this appears to be a fairly normal working class childhood for the period, but William's four wives and the speed with which he mostly married the next after the previous wife's death could point to something a little out of the ordinary, or even sinister.

Clarity is gained when it becomes more obvious that the family were early converts to Mormonism. William's brother Samuel had left the Trowbridge area for Utah and Salt Lake City in the early 1850s, and their father Edward and other siblings were also known to have been members of that church.

Five years before Mary's birth there were around 50,000 Mormons in the UK. The earliest establishment of Mormon worship in Wiltshire was in the mid-1840s at Steeple Ashton, just outside Trowbridge, which fits with where the family were based. Mormons, as it was a fairly new faith with different interpretations and customs from established Church of England practices or even non-conformist groups, met with a fair amount of suspicion and stigma in their community.

At that time the church had not yet renounced polygamy, so it is possible that William and his wives may have had arrangements that were not recognised in the law of the time.

Growing up in this community, wherever you were based, could not have been easy for Mary and her siblings. Indeed, a great many Mormons emigrated to Utah from the Steeple Ashton area in the later part of the 19th century, having faced persecution. It is therefore no surprise that Mary's choices in adulthood flew against society's norms, whether the family needed the money or not.

The family settled at Drynham, to the south of Trowbridge – a town with many cloth mills – during Mary's teens, and then into the town centre itself. She married Frederick Pepler, another weaver, in 1878 when she was around 19. Her father and stepmother and siblings were still in the area at the time, but they shortly emigrated to Utah themselves, leaving Mary behind. Her wedding doesn't appear to have taken place in Mormon premises, however, as they married in a non-conformist chapel.

Frederick, a cloth worker who had been brought up purely in Wiltshire, does not appear to have either shared Mary's faith or been particularly wedded to non-conformism. This is evident in that their first son, Thomas, who was well on the way by the time they married, had a Church of England baptism in Trowbridge.

Thomas, Mary's first born, did not live very long. He was dead within a month of birth. The same fate awaited her second child, Rosa Augusta, who followed just over a year later – though she managed to last three months. Throughout, Mary worked at the cloth mill, alongside Frederick. She was often given in records as a weaver, which would have been one of many people – men and women, married or single – who wove cloth on mechanised looms. Mary's weaving job would have been to push the shuttle back and forth in the warp and weft of the stretched yarn, and to create a densely packed tight cloth from the fibres which could then be used to make clothing and other textile products.

Her third child, a daughter named Rose, was the first to survive babyhood. By the time of the 1881 census she was three months old and living with her parents in a two-up, two down property in the southern part of Trowbridge. Even this early in her babyhood, Mary was still working as a woollen spinner, attached to one of the many nearby mills. A woollen spinner in this period would probably have been in charge of a spinning mule machine, which span multiple rovings of wool into yarn at a time by twisting and winding the fibres into cones. This produced a consistent yarn for the weavers in the cloth mill, further along the textile process.

She probably kept tiny babies with her, wrapped to her chest and breastfeeding on demand as she worked. Then as the child became more mobile and independent they would have been left with someone else. Mary's next two children, Laura and Frederick, also survived early

childhood, but a third daughter – Florence – did not, dying in the winter
of 1886 aged around 5 months.

Mary's husband Frederick, who later worked as an engine cleaner,
died shortly afterwards in early February, aged 32, leaving her cloth work
as the only means of support for her and her three surviving children.
Another baby, Herbert, followed in the Spring of 1887. Mathematics
would indicate that he was not Frederick's child, since he was born 13
months after his father's death, but he bore Frederick's surname. In
later life, when he signed up for the marines, he added a year to his age
– but since this would put his birth at barely seven months after that of
Florence, it does not work out. Exactly who Herbert's father was is lost to
time.

Around a year later, Mary's daughters Rose and Laura entered the
Union Workhouse at nearby Semington. Day books of entries have not
survived, so their records of entry come from the workhouse school.
It seems likely that Mary also entered, along with sons Frederick and
Herbert, who were too young for schooling, but no record survives of
this. To have at least some of the family in the workhouse means that she
was struggling financially to keep going.

Four years later though, Mary had come to Chippenham to work in
the Waterford Cloth Mill there and can be found on the 1891 census in
Westmead Lane, close to the mill itself. Her two surviving sons were with
her, but her daughters were not. Both still remained in the workhouse,
and had been baptised from there too. In addition, there was a new baby,
Walter, from her second husband Jacob Hancock – another worker at the
cloth mill. However, there is no formal record of their marriage evident.
Jacob had also been married before – his first wife Elizabeth died in
1888 – and Mary inherited six step-children. Despite a new baby, she was
following her regular pattern of working in the cloth mill. The fact that
both daughters were still in the workhouse meant that there was not
enough money coming in to support their upkeep.

Like the Trowbridge mills that Mary had worked in beforehand,
the Waterford Mill was water-driven to power the machines. An inlet of
water from the river Avon ran into a tunnel that arose on the far side
of Westmead Lane (sometimes called Factory Lane), and that body of
water was utilised for its force. The mid-19th century had seen that mill
– as Pocock and Rawlings – celebrated for superfine cloth that had been
exhibited at the Great Exhibition in 1851, but that that partnership
dissolved in the 1860s. Pocock still had control while Mary worked there

though, and the mill had a lasting reputation for fine quality woven wool cloth. Employees were taken on an annual trip, and the company would support new ideas for improving the town – for example, they provided the set up for the town swimming baths on the river Avon as Queen Victoria's Diamond Jubilee gift in 1897.

After Walter, Mary had five more children, taking her personal total of pregnancies to 14 and her combined total with Jacob's first family included to 20 children. The first after Walter was Florence, then Wilfrid (named after her brother, and who only lived a few months) then Wilfred, Lily, Ernest and William. William, the youngest, born in 1902 when she was around 43, again did not survive early childhood. So, although Mary had given birth to 14 children, she had only nine that lived past infancy.

Throughout all these pregnancies Mary continued to work in the cloth mill. As a weaver she would have worked a power loom in the late 19th century. These were intricate, if quite dangerous, machines by this stage which provided a consistent quality of cloth. On her looms, she would have been in charge of various processes driven by a harness (the main harness mender at this mill was another woman – Ellen Hillman), keeping the pointed flying shuttle's quill wound with enough yarn to form the weft as it shot back and forth across the warp yarns to build up the fabric, and battening (or pressing) the threads to condense them. These processes had been being developed on a more and more industrial scale as the 19th century progressed, and as Mary's career had continued she would have seen more innovation in the process – even if safety and care for the operators wasn't considered.

Back at home, one of her earlier daughters, Laura, came to live with the new family and worked at the nearby Nestles condensed milk factory. The other daughter from the workhouse seems to disappear – but may have been known as Annie rather than Rose, so could be in records under a different name. Her husband Jacob Hancock, who was also a hard worker, also sometimes worked at the cloth mill, but in addition worked as a carter for a local coal merchant. He is known to have been quite politically active, taking his children to see future Prime Minister Lloyd George speak in around 1903. His father was also living on Westmead Lane, which was known for parcels of poor-quality housing that would often flood on the ground floor when the river was high, so it is possible that he helped out with childcare for Mary and Jacob's children. Most of the children worked in local industries as they grew up – the cloth mill, and the milk factory invariably.

In 1910, at the age of 53, Mary died. Her daughters Florence and Laura, aged 17 and 21 respectively, therefore took on much of the household and care for the children, as Jacob continued to work for another three years until his own death. Two of her sons, Walter and Frederick were killed in the First World War, and the rest of her children all worked hard throughout their lives – mostly around Chippenham. It's her daughter Florence Hancock that is best remembered however, being extremely active around workers' rights, and an eventual president of the TUC. She was later made a Dame.

References

Adams, C (1982) *Ordinary Lives*, Virago Press
Bath Chronicle and Weekly Gazette, 26 June 1851 *The Great Exhibition*
Birmingham Daily Gazette, 4 August 1949 *Woman Member: Miss Florence Hancock*
BBC News (19.10.2021) *Dame Florence Hancock honoured with Chippenham blue plaque*, at https://www.bbc.co.uk/news/uk-england-wiltshire-58956315 (accessed 2/7/2023)
England and Wales: Birth, Marriage and Death Records, held by Ancestry.co.uk
England and Wales: Christening Index 1530-1980, held by Ancestry.co.uk

Eppich, C H (2011) *Remembering Family: The Hardings of Trowbridge, Wiltshire, England* http://infoquench.blogspot.com/2011/05/harding-of-trowbridge-wiltshire-england.html (accessed 2.7.2023)

Daniell, J.J (1894), *The History of Chippenham*, R F Houlston

Duffus, J (2018), *The Women Who Built Bristol 1184-2018*, Tangent Books

Illustrated London News, 7 June 1851, *Woollen and worsted fabrics*

Jefferies, S (1987), *A Chippenham Collection*, Chippenham Civic Society

Portsmouth Evening News, 23 January 1958 *New Remploy Directors*

UK census collection, held by Ancestry.co.uk

Western Daily Press, 4 April 1867, *Partnerships dissolved*

Wiltshire, England, Church of England Births and Baptisms 1813-1916, held by Ancestry.co.uk

Wiltshire, England, Church of England Deaths and Burials, 1813-1916, held by Ancestry.co.uk

Wiltshire, England, Church of England Marriages and Banns, 1754-1916, held by Ancestry.co.uk

Annie Peyton

ANNIE PEYTON'S FATHER'S position – a reverend with the West African Mission supported by the Church Mission Society – led to her unusual place of birth for a British Victorian woman. Both she and her older sister Mary were born in Freetown, the capital city of Sierra Leone, as their parents had gone out to help educate and convert the local residents to Christianity. The sisters, however, were packed off to boarding school in England incredibly young, ultimately growing up separately from their parents. In Annie's case this perhaps led to life-long mental health difficulties apparently on the streets of Chippenham, and a long stint in the Wiltshire County Lunatic Asylum in Devizes.

She was born in 1847. Her father Reverend Thomas Peyton had been stationed in Sierra Leone – at this stage a British colony – since 1837, returning to the UK only rarely, and was responsible for setting up the Freetown Grammar School in 1845. He was the first principal, with Annie's mother Maria running the girls' section of the school. A profile picture from the school, attributed to be Thomas Peyton, indicates that he may have been of mixed heritage though nominally European. However, one of the following principals, James Quaker, is claimed to be the first Sierra Leonean headteacher of the school, so this may be erroneous.

The idea of the grammar school was that by educating the people of Sierra Leone in a manner similar to that taught in 'civilised' Western

Europe, the boys would therefore serve as a beacon for the spread of Christianity in the country. To achieve this, pupils were taught a rigorous British education of the time – all aspects of English grammar and composition, Greek and Roman history, Bible and English history, arithmetic, geography, classics and mathematics. The pupils all had to convert to Christianity to receive this education.

The girls' section of the school, opened slightly later in 1845, aimed at giving a higher degree of education to 'those promising native girls, drawn from the village schools, who might afterwards be employed as teachers and school-mistresses.'

Annie's parents reputedly compared their students – who included sons of tribal chiefs – favourably to English students during a time when European racial prejudice against Africans was extremely high.

However, even their liberal-for-the-time views and their success with the school did not stretch to the education of their own children or them sharing in the instruction given to the Sierra Leone students.

Rather than being brought up alongside them, Annie's parents brought her and Mary – who was seven years her senior – back to London to be educated. They were on a period of leave from Sierra Leone in 1849, and spent part of that time raising funds for their mission, but evidently returned to Africa without their daughters. The girls were housed at the Missionary Children's Home in Islington, alongside children of others serving the Church Mission Society, and can be found there on the 1851 census. Annie was only four on that census, so at an extremely young age would have been separated from her parents as they travelled thousands of miles away.

The missionary home was a temporary measure, founded in 1849, and provided accommodation for around 50 children – all from similar backgrounds and separated from their parents. It was run by a clergyman and his wife, who – although clearly competent in spiritual matters – must have been spread very thin *in loco parentis*. The society started work on a more permanent premises in later 1851, completed in 1853, and it's likely that Annie and Mary were moved there with the rest of the children. This new premises housed around 100 children. Most of the children in the home had been born in various stations in India, but a few entered the world in Africa or South America.

In the summer of 1853, their father died in Sierra Leone, after a three-week fever, and their mother appears to have come home to the UK – although she did have business still in Africa and returned periodically over the next few years. She then took up the parental duties for Annie and Mary again, moving them to Minchinhampton in Gloucestershire and the rural life in which she herself had grown up. This was a far cry from the sultry climbs of Sierra Leone, where she had paid a worker from the local cotton gin a farthing for every cockroach he could catch in her house.

In later life, Annie's mother described her as a sharp and intelligent child, but it is unclear exactly how much time she spent in her company. Older sister Mary went to reside with relatives of her father for a while in Gloucestershire, while Annie appears to have lived with her mother. She also boarded at a private school in Weston-super-Mare for a time in her teens, spending further time away from home, which would have been intended to finish her education.

At some point in the 1870s, the family – Annie, Mary, and their mother Maria – moved to Chippenham. They took up residence in fashionable St Paul's Street, which had an array of recently-built quite grand (for the time) houses, and lived off Maria's inheritance from her husband and anything she earned from the Church Missionary Society.

According to medical records, around 1874 Annie suffered a prolonged gastric fever, which was said to have left her mentally weak. The family moved from their original Chippenham house to another round the corner at Landsend. Two years later, while her mother was out of the country, she was sent to the care of her maternal aunt in London, while there, aged in her late 20s, she had a love affair that sadly ended, but was said to have 'conducted herself well' for the duration, as might be expected from a good Christian girl from her background.

However, it was this experience – combined with the ill health that had plagued her since her fever, that seems to have exacerbated a mental health breakdown for Annie. She began writing letters filled with delusions that were sent to family and friends. She insisted that neighbours were passing evil thoughts to her by extra-sensory projection, and was afraid that someone was trying to injure her. Another delusion was that she had once died and come back to life again. She also wrote out texts of scriptures and would pass them to people in the street. She slept badly and lost weight.

Her aunt referred Annie to Bethlem Hospital in London in the July of 1876, where she was described as the 'orphan daughter of a clergyman' and diagnosed with melancholia via unceasing debility. Melancholia, in Victorian terms, generally meant depression and low spirits. The hospital records describe her as a 'small thin individual with very dry skin', who spent most of the day sewing. They also note that she wished her mother to keep moving house. Today there are many different treatments available for the illness Annie had, but back then very little was known about how to approach mental health.

Upon her mother's return to the UK, Annie was released from Bethlem and put under her care – which is given as 'special reasons' in her case notes. They returned to their life in Chippenham. However, Annie's illness soon became too much for her mother to cope with, and she was admitted initially to the workhouse – where she threw things and attacked an attendant – and then to the Wiltshire County Asylum at Roundway, near Devizes in the summer of 1878.

Here records show that Annie's problems had exacerbated since her removal from Bethlem. She was exhibiting symptoms of pica – eating soap, pig swill and unmentionable things from wastebaskets – and having no concern for her personal hygiene. She would also become violent and begin breaking household objects. This was now classed as mania. Her delusions and melancholia continued, and she often did not eat properly or at all, resulting in extreme thinness and weight loss.

The asylum considered that she was in good physical health, had been well off and had led a moral and temperate life.

Her mother briefly attempted to remove her from the asylum again in 1881, insisting in a heart-felt letter that she could cope and that her 'darling Annie' would be better off at home, but it appeared that the burden on Maria and Mary was too great, and Annie returned to Roundway around three months after she left, with little change in her condition reported. She would often keep her eyes covered, and repeat the same phrases.

Her mother died in Chippenham in 1886, while living at Landsend, and was buried at the town's St Paul's Church. Her sister Mary left the area after her mother's death. Annie remained in the asylum, with no reduction in symptoms and no successful treatment for a further 32 years. She died in her sixties of pneumonia, in early January 1914, and was reportedly severely underweight at that time.

References

Atlas, Saturday 23 July 1853, *Sierra Leone*
Bradford, M (2023) *The Sierra Leone Grammar School – the first secondary school in Sub- Saharan Africa!*, at https://shwenshwen.com/the-sierra-leone-grammar-

school-the-first-secondary-school-in-sub-saharan-africa/ (accessed 26
     November 2023)
C. Magbaily Fyle (2023) *The Grammar School and Education in Sierra Leone*, at
     https://slgsaanase.org/history-of-sierra-leone-grammar-school/ (accessed 26
     November 2023)
Case books and papers of Wiltshire County Lunatic Asylum, held by Wiltshire
     and Swindon History Centre.
Church Mission Society (2023) *Our Story*, at https://churchmissionsociety.org/
     about/our-story/ (accessed 26 November 2023)
England and Wales: Birth, Marriage and Death Records, held by Ancestry.co.uk
England and Wales: Christening Index 1530-1980, held by Ancestry.co.uk
Higginbotham, P (2023) *Children's Homes: Church Missionaries' Home,
     Islington/Limpsfield Common*, at https://www.childrenshomes.org.uk/
     ChurchMissionaries/index.shtml (accessed 26 November 2023)
Jefferies, S (1987), *A Chippenham Collection*, Chippenham Civic Society
London, Bethlem Hospital Patient Admission Registers And Casebooks 1683-
     1932, held by Findmypast.co.uk
Marke, Rev. C. (2018) *Origin of Wesleyan Methodism in Sierra Leone and History of
     its Missions*, First Fruits Press
Sibthorpe, A. B. C., (1970) *History of Sierra Leone*, Frank Cass and Company
UK census collection, held by Ancestry.co.uk
UK, Lunacy Patients Admission Registers, 1846-1921, held by Ancestry.co.uk
Walker, Rev. S A (1847), *The Church of England Mission in Sierra Leone: Including
     an Introductory Account of That Colony and a Comprehensive Sketch of the Niger
     Expedition in the Year 1841*, Seeley, Burnside and Seeley
West Briton and Cornwall Advertiser, Friday 10 May 1850, *Church Missionary
     Society*
Wiltshire Asylum Registers, 1789-1921, held by Findmypast.co.uk
Wiltshire, England, Church of England Deaths and Burials, 1813-1922, held by
     Ancestry.co.uk

Ida Hony or Gandy

A CAMPAIGNER AND activist for women's education, and later a playwright and author, Ida Gandy, née Hony's roots were very much in her beloved Wiltshire.

Born in 1885, she grew up in Bishop's Cannings, a village in the middle of Wiltshire, just outside Devizes, as the third of seven children (including a set of twins) of the village vicar Charles William Hony and his rather-unconventional wife. The fact that she was a vicar's daughter means that her exact time of birth is recorded alongside her baptism (2.40am).

She later recounted tales of her not-particularly straight-laced Victorian childhood in a memoir, *A Wiltshire Childhood*. One of these involved the whole tribe of her siblings regularly running about the village bare-footed and exacting the ridicule of some passing gypsies. The gypsies' reaction incensed their nurse so much that she insisted all the children return home and put on their Sunday best stockings and shoes, to be paraded in front of the travelling folk. However, when the children returned the gypsies had retreated to their tents for the night and the nurse's efforts were in vain.

The memoir further recounts that her mother, Annie Elizabeth née Lewin, was a writer, and appeared to have not too much care for the strict conventions of the day, leaving Ida and her siblings to roam the area as a gang – swimming in the canal, climbing the church roof, and wandering all over the local Wiltshire downlands. Ida and one of her younger sisters even went on a riding tour alone for three days, spending one night sleeping in a barn. Their household appears comfortable, with a whole complement of domestic staff to help the family, which would mean her mother had more time to write instead of child-rearing.

> At an age when such a thing was almost unheard of among well-to-do people, she let us go barefoot through the greater part of the year, regardless of all the compassionate outcry of all the old ladies.

When other little girls were wearing petticoats and frilly drawers, she anticipated fashion and put us into serge knickers to match our frocks. And she liked to dress us in clothes of her own design. The result, if my memory serves me, was sometimes charming and sometimes so odd that the other children of the neighbourhood would mock at us; but at least these garments were always original. Also, she gave us an amount of freedom that was undreamed of among most children of our age. From very early years we were encouraged to go unattended in the fields and over the downs. In other ways too, she urged us to be independent and take our own line through life, and if later on these lines did not always meet with her approval she accepted them philosophically.'

(A Wiltshire Childhood)

Ida was also a keen archer in her youth, taking part in mixed doubles matches for the Wiltshire Society of Archers when she was around 20.

When Ida was in her early 20s and still living at home, her father's church position moved to another village in Wiltshire – Woodborough – which was closer to the rapidly-growing Swindon. It was here that she became involved in the work of the Workers' Educational Association (WEA), which was initially set up in London in 1903 but had enthusiastically been taken up in Swindon in subsequent years by Swindon politician and county councillor Reuben George. The WEA was founded to further the education of people who had left school and were already in the workforce, aiming to bring new skills to the whole population, with focus on the working class. This was part of a drive in the Edwardian age to improve and progress society away from the perceived social problems of the 19th century.

Ida, in the face of considerable opposition from the locals, set up the first village branch of the WEA in Woodborough. This endeavour was supported by Reuben George, who was a committed socialist and pacifist, and a believer in breaking down class barriers through education. He was elected to Swindon Town and Wiltshire County Councils, and worked hard in both positions serving on committees and societies. Much of his involvement with the WEA involved local walks and rambles, where participants learned as they went. Ida took part in these in as part of her involvement with the association.

The WEA offered lectures and tutorial classes, which could be attended by anyone from an iron worker to a carpet weaver, to a wool sorter or a clerk. Initially lectures could be attended by hundreds of people at a time, but the tutorial classes were limited to 24 students at a time and met weekly, following a curriculum which promoted the higher education of both men and women. Ida's work for the organisation would have involved the administration of these lessons, and would have helped to promote the education of women within this aim.

Her involvement was a step towards her lifelong drive towards social reform, and was followed by another – a short semi-academic stay in Oxford with a university family to hone her skills, and then a subsequent move to London to undertake social work, alongside her work with the WEA. Indeed, on the 1911 census she was in London, lodging with a female tutor in sociology and called herself a social worker – a fairly unusual choice of a career for a woman of her background. At home her branch of the WEA flourished, with her parents and siblings also attending meetings.

The WEA Women's Advisory Committee was founded in 1907, which aimed to investigate providing adult education classes for women. The first WEA women's officer, Alice Wall, was appointed in 1910 as a special organiser. The role involved encouraging the WEA branches to add women into their committees as representatives of women's organisations, and to form women's committees and sections. Alice Wall married in 1912 and resigned her position, and Ida was appointed the second WEA women's officer. She was 27.

Ida built on Alice's work. Women's committees and sections had been formed in London, Reading and Birmingham in 1910, with five more established in 1911. By 1914-15 Ida had managed to increase this to 34 of the 179 branches at that time. She was known to have been energetic at this task, developing women's sections and committees and promoting classes, lectures and study circles. Much of this work was in London, where she was based at headquarters at Red Lion Square and in 1914-15 had 50 women's lecture programmes organised, but she also travelled to other branches and conferences elsewhere in the country and worked with other women in the organisation, so the scope of the work was much larger than that.

The role also put her in a position of improving the lives of women when the women's suffrage campaign was at its height. In 1912 she wrote:

> If the WEA is to gain any substantial victory in its campaign against
> ignorance and injustice, men and women must be fighting side by side.

Their cause, their interests are inseparably bound together. Neither party can march by itself without endangering both its own safety, and that of the party it has left, and if one ceases to make progress, the other is held back too; so, of all the special efforts the WEA has to make today, perhaps none is more important than the special effort it is making on behalf of women.

It was at one WEA position – in Rotherfield Peppard in Oxfordshire about three years later – that she met and fell in love with the community doctor Thomas Gandy. As married women of her class were not really supposed to have jobs (or at the very least not admit to them), she resigned her post with the WEA and did not even acknowledge her working life on her wedding certificate, when they married in the middle of the First World War. She was 30, which was widely considered a late marriage for women at the time.

With Ida's resignation the WEA executive decided to reassess the function of the Women's Advisory Committee. Against the background of the First World War, some of the functions went to the London women's committee, and the paid role of a women's officer was axed. The ideas were not really picked up again for decades.

Meanwhile, Ida settled into life as a doctor's wife in Oxfordshire. As a doctor, her husband was in a reserved occupation and therefore excused conscription – so did not go to war. Ida gave birth to two sons – Christopher and Robin – in quick succession in the years that followed.

It was as part of this life that Ida, who had followed her mother's talents and had been a compulsive writer since childhood, began to write in earnest. As her children grew, she started as a playwright in the 1920s, penning several works for children before working on dramas and comedies for adult groups. At the tail end of the 1920s she gave birth to her third child – a daughter, Gillian – nearly ten years after her second son. She continued to write plays, sometimes directing them or producing them with amateur and semi-professional companies, and several were broadcast by the BBC on the home service in the early days of radio. One, a comedy called *Lardy Cake*, referred to a popular Wiltshire baked product, and others made reference to occurrences in her Wiltshire childhood. She also started writing books, among them *A Wiltshire Childhood*, a lively account of her early years, which was published in 1929.

The family moved to Clunbury in Shropshire in 1930, where Ida's plays continued to be written and performed by the village players, and her two sons went to study at university while her daughter went to boarding school. She also wrote and broadcast about Shropshire life – several plays, a children's book, and notably a book called *An Idler on the Shropshire Borders* which reminisced much later and was published in 1970. Her rambling in the early days of the Woodborough WEA branch seems to have stuck with her, and she was known to have loved walking and exploring nature at every chance she got.

During World War Two in Clunbury she was very active in the local Women's Institute, and gave considerable voluntary time to various good causes including working with evacuees from the cities. Writing took a bit of a back seat for Ida at this time.

Her husband Thomas retired at the end of World War Two, and they moved to Cerne Abbas in Dorset – but Ida was widowed about three years later in 1948. She began to travel the world, as her family had spread out and her eldest son Christopher was now working as a diplomat and was posted to far flung places. With his work stationing him abroad, she went to Iran, Portugal, Libya and the USA. Her second son Robin was an academic mathematician, while daughter Gillian was a physician specialising in pioneering neo-natal care.

She moved back to Wiltshire around 1950, and settled in the village of Aldbourne, and it was here that she properly returned to writing. In the early 1960s she researched and published a book on Bishop's Cannings, the village she grew up in – *Round About The Little Steeple*. This was followed by *Holidays With The Aunts*, a book detailing holidays with her father's sisters, five spinster aunts in the New Forest area of Hampshire.

After *An Idler On the Shropshire Borders* was published, Ida prepared her final book - an intricately researched history of Aldbourne, *The Heart of a Village*. That appeared in 1975, when she was well into her 80s. She remained at the heart of village life until she died in 1977, and was buried in Aldbourne churchyard.

References

Alcock, G (year unknown) *WEA South West: A Heritage of Learning*, at www.weaheritageoflearning.org (accessed 01/10/2023)

Common Cause, 4 September 1914, *The Worker's Education Association*

Daily Mirror, 8 November 1933 *Midland Regional*

Devizes and Wilts Advertiser, 21 September 1911, *Woodborough*

Dobson, R (2019) *Border Crossings: Then and Now in the Welsh Marches* Grosvenor House Publishing

Edinburgh Evening News, 15 February 1932 *Good Production Lacking*

England and Wales: Birth, Marriage and Death Records, held by Ancestry.co.uk

England and Wales: Christening Index 1530-1980, held by Ancestry.co.uk

Fraser, W (1995), *Learning from Experience. Empowerment or Incorporation? National Institute of Adult Continuing Education (England and Wales)* at https://files.eric.ed.gov/fulltext/ED396139.pdf (accessed 01/10/2023)

Gandy, I (1929) *A Wiltshire childhood*. London: Allen & Unwin

Gandy, I (1970) *An idler on the Shropshire borders*. Shrewsbury: Wilding

Hampshire Advertiser, 4 November 1933 *Midland Regional*

Hartlepool Northern Daily Mail, 18 April 1942 *Monday Home Service Programme*

Northampton Chronicle and Echo, 9 November 1950, *Soap The Furniture*

Northern Whig, 30 November 1929 *A Wiltshire Childhood*

Oxford Chronicle and Reading Gazette, 12 August 1927 *World Brotherhood*

Roberts, S (ed) (2003) *A Ministry of Enthusiasm: Centenary Essays on the Workers' Educational Association*, Pluto Press

Stockton Herald, South Durham and Cleveland Advertiser, 4 October 1913 *To Educate the Workers*

UK census collection, held by Ancestry.co.uk

Wiltshire, England, Church of England Births and Baptisms 1813-1916, held by Ancestry.co.uk

Wiltshire, England, Church of England Deaths and Burials, 1813-1916, held by Ancestry.co.uk

Walker, Ann (2014) *Women overcoming disadvantage through education*, at https://

annwalkerwea.wordpress.com/2014/06/ (accessed 01/10/2023)

Western Daily Press, 6 July 1915 *Workers Educational Association, Ramble in the Hanham District*

Wiltshire Times and Trowbridge Advertiser, 26 April 1924 *Easter Sightseers*

Margaret Bruce Long or Giffard or Griffin

WEALTHILY-BORN MARGARET DID everything that was expected of a young woman in the early 20th century – supported her family's political and social ambitions, married well and produced a clutch of children. But her love of her beloved German Shepherd dogs took her out of that role and into that of a war hero. She played a vital role in search and rescue during the Second World War, saving the lives of 21 people when she and her working dogs managed to locate them in the rubble of the doodlebug blitz.

Training dogs to find buried people was an incredibly new (and incredibly dangerous) thing in the 1940s, and Margaret was at the forefront of this practice – and even was awarded a gong for bravery.

Co-incidentally, a house she spent some of her early life living in later played an important part in saving people's lives too, although long after she left. Rowden Hill House, just beneath Chippenham's St Andrew's Hospital, was accommodation for nursing staff in the 1960s and 1970s, and is now in need of some tender loving care itself. Margaret, who was born in Marlborough in 1889, lived there with her family from before 1909 until late 1913, but also lived in the USA, New Zealand and Southern Rhodesia (now Zimbabwe).

Early photographs of Margaret often show her with dogs, as, like many women of her class and means, she had room for several at home and doted on them. Her family had moved to Rowden Hill House to further her father's political ambitions – Robert (Bob) Chaloner Critchley Long came from a landowning Wiltshire family and had been selected as the Conservative and Unionist Party candidate for the West Wiltshire (at that time you did not need to live in your constituency) for the first 1910 general election, held that January.

Prior to this, they'd lived in Ludlow, but as they arrived in the town Margaret's older sister Muriel had married, so didn't join the family. Instead, Margaret and her younger sister Joan became part of the Chippenham branch of the Women's Unionist and Tariff Reform Association.

This group, from the days before women could vote, were a way some women could get involved in politics and have an influence on the way men voted. The Tariff Reform League, of which they were an offshoot, formed in 1903, was effectively a pressure group promoting British empire industry and products over those imported from elsewhere. The Unionist part of their name meant that they opposed home rule in Ireland. These values were extremely popular and aligned with the Conservative party, who at the time were known as the Conservative and Unionist party. One of the key tenets of the Women's Unionist and Tariff Reform Association was that women's engagement in political life was vital, both as citizens and as consumers of goods. This was part of a wider evolving of thought which was part of the process of women gaining a vote.

Despite Margaret's involvement, her father did not win the West Wiltshire seat in January 1910, and did not stand again in the subsequent general election in December 1910, which was called to attempt to pass a mandate.

An announcement of Margaret's impending marriage was made in the society papers in March 1911 when she was 22. Her intended was Andrew Reynold Uvedale Corbett, of Crabwell Hall in Cheshire. For whatever reason, this marriage did not take place. Andrew never married, and instead became an antique dealer in Hampshire. The end of the engagement got a quiet mention in *The Gentlewoman* in March 1912.

Margaret's family remained at Rowden Hill until late 1913, when her parents moved them to Northcliffe House, just outside Bradford on Avon. It was from this house that Margaret actually did get married, in January 1914. Her new husband was Jack Giffard, a member of a prestigious family from Lockeridge, near Marlborough.

Like Margaret and many other members of the landed class, Jack was also keen on animals – dogs and horses particularly. He was serving with the Royal Horse Artillery at the time, and as such might have expected to see action when the First World War began later that year. He played an active part in the early part of the conflict but after his twin brother was killed in action in autumn 1914 he stepped back and was specially employed by the war office from 1915.

Margaret seems to have regarded her dogs on an equal footing as her forthcoming children, focusing on their breeding just as much as her own. She had their first daughter, Violet, in 1915, when they were living at Long Ashton just south of Bristol. She was pregnant with their next daughter – Sybelle – when Jack was sent to the USA on war business of the Anglo-Russian sub-committee in the Autumn of 1915, without her. Sybelle entered the world in Charlton in Kent in April 1916, presumably close to where Jack had been garrisoned before he left the country. She was then baptised near Marlborough, as Margaret had presumably brought her daughters back to Jack's family in Wiltshire for support caring for them while her husband was away.

In June 1916, around two months after giving birth to Sybelle, Margaret arrived in New York to reunite with Jack. Neither baby Sybelle nor toddler Violet went with her, so they were cared for elsewhere. She spent two years in New York with Jack, and they arrived back after the war was over, in December 1918, with a third baby – Jacqueline – in tow.

In England, they lived at Shurnhold House at Melksham, but in reality it appears Jack spent very little time there as he's given as going back and forth to New York on ships over the next couple of years. Margaret seems to have left the children under the care of staff and spent time elsewhere too: on the 1921 census she was visiting her younger sister Joan in Westminster. Joan had been married and divorced by this time, and was working as a dressmaker's model.

After this, Margaret and the children (and Jack, when he was in the country), lived first in Amersham in Buckinghamshire, and then in Putney. About this time, Margaret started breeding dogs seriously, and another daughter, Eleanor, joined them in 1923. Shurnhold House was passed to someone else.

It's while they were in Putney that a glimpse of Margaret's life to come starts to shine through. There's a newspaper reference to a Mrs Giffard being involved in demonstrating the skills of working dogs, alongside a police dogs demonstration, in January of 1924 at Crystal Palace. The article radiates some excitement at the potential for the use of working dogs, since this was a particularly new idea anywhere other than the North East transport police forces who had been using dogs since around 1906. She was also an honorary secretary of the Alsatian Sheep, Police and Army Dog Society around this time. Her kennel name, Crumstone, was breeding dogs in the London area in the 1920s.

However, there's no further mention of Mrs Giffard connected with dog training after this, and Jack seems to have decided to become a farmer in the newly-formed British colony of Southern Rhodesia, so left for Africa in September 1925. Margaret's father appears to have gone out there slightly earlier, so the plan may have been for the rest of the family to come and join him and become prosperous out there. At some point after that Margaret and her daughters followed him, and both her sisters ended up there too. Jack went back and forth between various African ports and England several times over the next few years, but Margaret never seemed to be with him.

Mrs Giffard has one last mention at a Catholic wedding in Harare in 1927, where her two younger daughters were bridesmaids, and then there is no more mention of Margaret under that name.

Jack remarried in Penhalonga, Southern Rhodesia, in 1933, so their relationship had come to an end. Her father died in 1938, in Wraxall, Southern Rhodesia, and – alongside leaving his housekeeper £200 for looking after his grandchildren – his will refers to Margaret as Margaret Bruce Griffin, so it appears that she had remarried too.

This marriage took place in New Zealand in 1930, to Harold Desmond Griffin. They returned to Britain in 1935 and settled in Sussex, where Harold worked as a farm manager and Margaret started her own boarding kennels. This marriage does not appear to have lasted either, as by the beginning of the Second World War Margaret was in Surrey, living on her own. She kept goats and poultry, and was training dogs for both war and the police.

Margaret was, by this stage, a renowned breeder and trainer of German Shepherd dogs, or Alsatians as they were known at the time. She attended various dog shows with her charges, and was becoming well known for the breed. She is also supposed to have provided a dog from her kennel for Hermann Goering before the war. German Shepherds had been favoured as police and working dogs since the Hull force – the first in the country to employ dogs – had decided to use them in 1923. Forces elsewhere in the country gradually became interested, and the Home Office had set up a committee to evaluated the use of dogs in policing in 1934, with a couple of labradors added to the Metropolitan force in 1935.

There were two schools training dogs for war work. The Army's War Dogs Training School was initially based at Aldershot, then at Ickenham and then in Hertfordshire. It started with just a few dogs

but by 1944 had capacity for 750 canines. Margaret became part of the
staff at the other school, the Ministry of Aircraft Production Guard
Dog School (MAPGDS), which was based at Woodfold near Gloucester.
This school had been founded in November 1941 by Lieutenant Colonel
Baldwin, and started with just 15 dogs. Two years later there were 665
dogs either training or working at Ministry of Aircraft Production (MAP)
sites throughout the UK. The MAPGDS was absorbed into the RAF Police
and retitled the RAF Police Dog Training School in 1944.

      While working with training police dogs was important in terms of
developing that relationship and the skills involved in policing, Margaret
and a couple of other trainers actually played a far more important part
in war work. She was involved in the instigation of training and using
dogs to locate and find people needing rescuing from disasters – bombs,
gas explosions and building collapses. The concept of search and rescue
dogs was an entirely new idea at the time.
      The dogs used for rescuing, however, while trained at these
schools, weren't those used by the military or police but instead tended
to be the personal dogs of these trainers.
      The story of how dogs came to be used for rescuing trapped people
from under rubble is rumoured to have come from Colonel Baldwin having

watched *The Siege of Stalingrad* at Cheltenham cinema which gave rise to
the idea that dogs – with their enhanced sense of smell – could be trained
to locate buried casualties. Indeed, the first documented rescue of an
avalanche victim located by an untrained dog occurred in 1937. Margaret
lit on the idea and started working on it with dogs from her kennels, and
recalled a couple of dogs that had previously been through the MAP school
to see if they could be retrained. One dog she retrieved from New Zealand.

They began working on commands and tells, and eventually gave
a demonstration to the Minister of Home Security where volunteers hid
themselves on bombed sites amid burning rags. The dogs had located
their targets within two minutes. The first dog to go into service was
Jet, who had been trained by Margaret. The dog started working on a
site that had been bombed by a V-1 attack in north London in October
1944, and was distracted by onlookers, but soon after that located three
deceased casualties after another attack at Purley.

After this, Margaret formed a team with two of her dogs – Irma
and Psyche – from her renowned Crumstone Kennel, and worked
alongside rescue teams throughout the doodlebug blitz, where V-1
flying bombs fell on London, to locate casualties buried under collapsed
buildings. Between them, Margaret and her dogs managed to locate
233 victims in the rubble, 21 of whom were still alive. They also located
buried pets alongside the humans.

Irma was particularly good at locating. She would change the
sound of her bark when she felt that a victim was still alive, and would
often not leave the site until the casualty was found. On one occasion it
took two days to unearth two girls, and Irma refused to leave. Another
tell from the dogs that indicated that someone was to be found was
for Psyche and Irma's ears to suddenly lie flat on their neck, and they
would also excitedly scratch at the remains of the houses if they believed
someone was alive.

Margaret, who attended the sites with the dogs in a blue-serge
civil defence great coat and a beret with a German Shepherd badge on
it, would also put her own safety at risk while working with her team
to rescue people. She appears to have been incredibly brave and stoical
about the work in hand. Extracts from her diary, which is believed to be
held by the Dogs' Trust, read:

> *11 and 12.11.1944.-* Rocket at Shooter's Hill. 20.05 hrs. Public House,
> Ambulance Depot and 2 offices. Put Irma on right away. Frightful mess.

Most of the casualties known to be in bar and billiard room of Pub but a
few 'unknowns' had to be located. Irma gave strong indication to right of
debris... Digging proceeded here and after 2 hours the bodies of 2 women
were recovered in the exact position, under approximately 7 feet of debris
below the dog's indication.'

21.11.1944 – Rocket on Walthamstowe (sic), 12.30 hrs. Arrived on
site 13.30 hrs. Four houses completely demolished, about twelve badly
knocked about. Things were made no easier by water pipes burst in all
directions and a bad gas leak under the debris. A smashed meter was
pouring gas into the rubble. Worked Irma. In spite of the stench of gas,
she indicated at a point at the back of the debris. From the front of the
building, she and I went right under the floors crawling on our stomachs
in water. She lay down here when we reached a point approximately
dead below the spot where she had indicated. Below this the bodies of a
woman and two children were buried 4ft under fine rubble and dust.

20.1.1945 – Call to Osborne Road, Tottenham at 21:00 hrs. In house
No.1 Irma found two live casualties. In No.2 Irma again gave good
indication just to one side of a fairly large and fierce fire burning through
collapsed house debris. Thick smoke rising here. Family of five found. In
No.3 a strong indication from Irma over the debris. Rescue found a live
cat.

Once the war came to an end in the spring of 1945, the direct
services of Psyche and Irma, and therefore Margaret, were no longer
needed with such urgency. However, their courage and wartime roles did
not go unrewarded. Irma had been awarded the Dickin Medal (a bravery
award for working animals during wartime) in January of 1945, and she
and Margaret took part in the victory celebrations on Pall Mall in June
1946, alongside the first rescue dog Jet. They were the only two dogs to
take part.

Margaret herself received the British Empire Medal in the 1946
New Year Honours, for her work training and working alongside the
dogs.

Away from her war work, both her sisters had died in Harare
(then known as Salisbury) during the war – Joan in 1941 and Muriel in
1943. The rest of the family also seem to have continued living in either
Southern Rhodesia or South Africa. Margaret's eldest daughter Violet,
had married, then divorced, a wildlife expert. She then married again.
Her third daughter Jacqueline married in India during the war, and

eventually moved to Australia. And fourth daughter Eleanor became a
nun in South Africa. However, there is no indication whether Margaret
ever went back to Southern Rhodesia to see them. Her ex-husband Jack
died in 1956, also in Southern Rhodesia.

Once the war was over, Margaret and her dogs returned to the
dog school at Gloucester, where Irma and Psyche demonstrated their
skills alongside another dog called Storm, who was also from Margaret's
Crumstone kennel and had appeared on screen in *Owd Bob* (1938). The
trainers, including Margaret, also began to investigate teaching their
dogs to search for victims in terrains other than rubble. Lieutenant
Colonel Baldwin arranged for three of the dogs to search a mine in
Cumbria after an explosion in 1947. The groundwork put in by Margaret
and other trainers during the war built the foundations for modern
search and rescue operations.

Later on, Margaret is known to have exhibited dogs from her
Crumstone kennel at Crufts Dog Show. There are pictures of her with
Irma and Psyche meeting children that she had rescued from rubble in
1945, at Crufts in 1950. Eventually Irma died, and was buried at the
PDSA Animal Cemetery in Ilford.

As for Margaret, after 1950 she mostly disappears from public
view. She continued to breed German Shepherds and train them when
necessary for different purposes, and would also have continued to
attend Crufts. She is known to have been based at Wallingford in
Oxfordshire in the early 1950s, and have lived alone. The 1961 Crufts
Catalogue has her entering German Shepherds in several categories, and
advertising her small Crumstone kennel at Goring-on-Thames in the
same pages, listing many winners in the UK and on the international
stage. Her dog Crumstone Strolch had won many prizes and had
starred in the films *Circus Friends* (1956), *Ill Met By Moonlight* (1957)
and Norman Wisdom's *Follow a Star* (1959). This probably meant that
Margaret would have attended film sets with her dogs while they
appeared on camera.

She died in Henley on Thames, in May 1972, aged 83. Her death
went unremarked upon in the newspapers. In a case of life following art,
the house where she spent some of her formative years - Rowden Hill
House in Chippenham - is now in disrepair and has most recently been
used for the training of police dogs, but at the time of writing has been
placed on sale.

References

Bath Chronicle and Weekly Gazette, 17 January 1914, *Marriage of Miss Margaret Long*

Bath Chronicle and Weekly Gazette, 7 January 1939, *Major Robert Long's Will - Bequests from £82,000 estate*

Brice O'Donnell, K (2019) *Doing Their Bit: The British Employment of Military and Civil Defence Dogs*, Helion & Company

Campbell, C (2014) *Bonzo's War: Animals Under Fire 1939 -1945*, Constable & Robinson

Campbell, C & Campbell, C (2015), *Dogs of Courage: When Britain's Pets Went to War 1939–45*, Corsair

Clifton Society, 23 September 1909, *Army and Navy notes*

Clifton Society, 23 March 1911, *Approaching marriages*

Crufts Official Catalogue 1961, *Crumstone Alsatians*

England and Wales: Birth, Marriage and Death Records, held by Ancestry.co.uk

England and Wales: Christening Index 1530-1980, held by Ancestry.co.uk

Jefferies, S (1987), *A Chippenham Collection*, Chippenham Civic Society

Kensington News and West London Times, 27 May 1927 *Livestock for sale etc*

Leeds Mercury, 10 May 1937, *Dogs*

Long, D (2012), *The Animals' VC: For Gallantry and Devotion: the PDSA Dickin Medal*, Preface Publishing

Somerset Guardian and Radstock Observer, 9 December 1955. *Funeral of well-known farmer*

The Gentlewoman, 2 March 1912. *Will not take place.*

The Sketch, 14 January 1914, *Crowns. Coronets. Courtiers*

The Tatler, 16 November 1927, *Round and about notes*

UK census collection, held by Ancestry.co.uk

Voluntary Service Gazette and Military Dispatch, Friday 9 February 1900. *Yeomanry Cavalry*

Western Daily Press, 15 January 1914. *A Wiltshire Wedding.*

Western Daily Press, 7 October 1938. *Somerset Major's death abroad*

Wiltshire Times and Trowbridge Advertiser, 9 October 1909. *The prospective Conservative candidate*

Elizabeth Prevett or Hayes or Clifford

WOMEN HAVE BEEN unexpectedly discovering that they are pregnant since time immemorable. However, if that pregnancy is unwelcome or unwanted, how they have reacted over the millennia is related to religious, cultural, temporal and societal factors.

In the mid-19th century, if you were poor and unmarried, you had stark options if you found yourself in this situation. An illegitimate child was a massive stigma in society which could have detrimental implications for your life thereafter, and for that of your child. Abortion was illegal if you were caught and the abortifacients available at this time could be dangerous and didn't always work, and there were huge religious implications for this option in a very God-fearing society. Another option was to have the baby and pass it off as someone else's – perhaps your mother might claim it as your younger sibling – but if you were on your own far from home that wasn't possible, and it'd be a rare family who could afford to take in another mouth to feed if the baby was offered for adoption. A final option, which some women took, was to conceal the pregnancy and to then either abandon or kill the baby when it arrived – which again was illegal, and had religious implications.

Elizabeth Hayes, née Prevett, a widow aged 31, faced this dilemma in 1870. She was living on her own with her two sons from her marriage in Lowden in Chippenham, a street-cum-village which was down-at-heel at the time, and had portions that were semi-rural, poor and crowded. Within a few years it would start to be redeveloped as railway workers' housing, but at the time Elizabeth's neighbours were labourers, hauliers, brickmakers, cloth factory workers, and she was working as a labourer and charwoman. This would have meant very low wages, and no particularly stable employment, and she really couldn't afford another mouth to feed.

Despite the economics, she could have insisted that the baby was legitimate and had been fathered by her dead husband. The trouble was, she'd already done that 15 months earlier when she'd given birth to a little boy she had baptised as Alfred, who didn't live long enough to have his birth registered. The fact that her husband Eli had actually passed away in 1865 would have made this completely impossible, and the true father of the child was either not interested or unavailable to support Elizabeth, but attempting to pass off this little boy as legitimate could have created a veneer of respectability even if everyone would have suspected the truth. So, finding herself pregnant again in the winter of 1870 meant that claiming that the new baby was also fathered by her dead husband would not have been an option.

It's unknown whether she tried any abortifacients – for example, rue was often employed in these situations – but if she did, they didn't work. Therefore, Elizabeth opted to conceal her pregnancy. This would have been easier than now, due to fuller skirts in women's outfits, and stays would also have helped. She was therefore able to continue working and go about daily life as normal. Whether the concealment was intended, or part of denial and mental health issues brought on by grief having lost a baby and a husband, is open to question. Concealing a pregnancy was not illegal at the time, but concealing a birth was, under the Offences against the Person Act 1861 – some of which legislation has not been repealed today. Therefore, she was on the road to committing an offence.

Technically, this wasn't her first offence. She and her husband Eli Hayes had lied on their marriage certificate about their ages. They'd married in Corsham in 1860, and Elizabeth would have been 21 – which was old enough to marry without a parents' permission under the law of the time. Eli, however, was 20 – which was under-age. He increased his age by a year, as did she. While this was an offence, this was a common occurrence, and was usually let slide. And it appears that they didn't admit to being married at first. A year later, on the 1861 census, Eli – who was a railway porter – was living away from Elizabeth and lodging in the High Wycombe area. He did admit to being married. She, on the other hand, does not appear under her married name, and could well be visiting farming friends of her parents in Sussex posing as an unmarried woman.

Elizabeth had grown up in Sussex, just outside modern-day Crawley and close to where Gatwick Airport now sits, and was the daughter of rather a prosperous farmer. She was one of the middle children of a family of at least 13, and at the time her father died in 1851 – when she was just 13 – she was living away from home and working

as a servant on another farm. Her mother appears to have not kept
the farm, and took up working as a monthly nurse to make ends meet.
Elizabeth and her siblings seem to have scattered on the wind.

Exactly where Elizabeth met Eli is unknown. He was a porter for
the Great Western Railway though, like his older brother Andrew before
him, so it may well have been at a station. At the time of their marriage
he was based at Paddington station, and she was possibly a servant at
Hartham House on the outskirts of Corsham. If, as suspected, they hid
their marriage for a while, it appears they reunited at some point in
1862. Their first son, Herbert, was born in High Wycombe in the early
part of 1863. The new family then moved to Oxfordshire, as next son
Charles was born in Thame in the spring of 1864.

They returned to Eli's home (he'd been brought up in the village
of Yatton Keynell, just outside Chippenham) to have Charles christened.
Here they stayed, as Eli died the following year aged just 25. His parents,
who were agricultural labourers, were in no position to support Elizabeth
and her sons. So, she moved to a cottage on Lowden in Chippenham and
took work where she could find it, which all led up to the concealment of
her pregnancy in 1870.

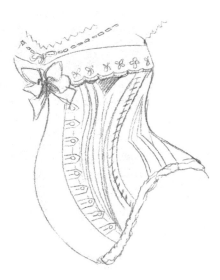

It appears that on 6th September that year Elizabeth took to her
bed and refused to see anyone except her two sons. This behaviour must
have been out of the ordinary, as her neighbours were suspicious, and

one decided to write to the local surgeon/doctor Dr Spencer outlining what they thought. Dr Spencer went to Elizabeth's home, found her in bed with her clothes on, and accused her of concealing a birth. She denied it, and refused to let him examine her.

Undeterred, he took the letter to the police and the following day police superintendent Mr Wiltshire visited Elizabeth. Confronted with the officials, and obviously realising that the game was up, she admitted that she'd given birth but the baby hadn't survived, and she'd concealed it all. The baby, a little girl (initial reports wrongly identified the child as male), was found wrapped in calico in a box at the foot of the bed. She had presumably been too ill since the birth to bury her daughter, or at least decide what to do next.

Elizabeth was taken into custody. Dr Spencer examined the dead child, and reached a verdict that the child had been suffocated by the umbilical cord around her neck during the birth, the result of having no-one to assist with labour. Therefore, Elizabeth was not charged with infanticide and her offence was the lesser one of concealing a birth. She was due to be charged when she recovered enough to face a court hearing. The register of births, marriages and deaths records the death of an unnamed female bearing Elizabeth's married surname in Chippenham at this time. Whether concealment followed by abandonment, or something worse, was what Elizabeth intended for the child, it's a situation she would not have gone into lightly, and is desperately sad that the community around her would not have supported her properly following the birth of another child.

She was held at Devizes prison until the case came to trial. She would have been held in a cell specially built for the use of women, dating from around 1841. Her sons went to live with her mother-in-law Sarah, who was widowed and working at Doncombe Paper Mill up the road in the village of Ford.

The trial, in late March 1871, saw Elizabeth plead guilty and say that she was very sorry that she had done it. Under the Offences Against The Person Act 1861 she could have faced up to two years in prison, but as the judge had found 'that there was no evidence of the destruction of the child', and had already served six months in prison, she was given another three months with hard labour. At Devizes Prison, which was the only prison in Wiltshire and was situated by the Kennet and Avon Canal, a prison term with hard labour would have included baking, cooking, cleaning and walking a treadmill to grind corn. Elizabeth completed her sentence in the summer of 1871, and would have reunited with her sons.

Rather surprisingly, the next record to feature her is another marriage. She married Thomas Clifford, a widower 35 years her senior, around nine months after leaving prison. Thomas's daughter Eliza had married her first husband Eli's brother Job in the winter of 1870, so Elizabeth would probably have known him before her prison term. He was widowed while she was concealing her pregnancy.

This was probably quite a canny move on Elizabeth's part. Thomas had a stable job as a small-scale farmer, and a clutch of children from his first marriage that were either grown up or close to becoming independent. And at around 70 he would not be expected to live much longer. Her sons would have lived with them, on his farm in Cricklade – a town in the very north of Wiltshire close to the border with Oxfordshire. Elizabeth gave birth a final time, to a daughter called Ellen, in 1873.

However, Thomas did have longevity. The 1881 census finds him as a farmer of 15 acres, employing one boy – probably his stepson Charles, who was living with them. Elizabeth, given her family background in farming, is given as a farmer's wife and undoubtedly had her own jobs on the land – but typically the enumerator has crossed out her occupation as she wasn't supposed to admit to it.

Thomas died in 1883, aged around 80. Exactly what happened to Elizabeth after that is unknown for a few years. She appears not to have continued at the farm, as it went to Thomas's son Henry from his previous marriage.

Her eldest son Herbert got married in the London area to a woman named Caroline in 1883. He would have been around 21. However, he and Caroline were witnesses to younger son Charles's very definitely underage wedding the same year – he married Emma, a woman from Minety, and claimed to be 22 but was actually around 19.

In 1887, her son Charles was convicted of arson, having tried to burn down a house he owned in Brinkworth, to defraud a fire insurance company. He received six years of penal servitude. He was imprisoned in Devizes initially, and then later was moved to Portland in Dorset. Exactly what happened to his wife during this time is unclear.

Elizabeth and her daughter Ellen are not visible on the 1891 census – Herbert was working as an oilman and building his family in Ealing while Charles was in prison. There is also no sign of them on prison records, nor in an asylum. They may have assumed a false name, or have had their details poorly recorded.

Charles, after his release from prison, went straight and set up a greengrocers' shop next door to Herbert in Ealing. He also married again, this time to Gertrude. Exactly what had happened to previous wife Emma is unknown. Reports of the arson mention that they had two children. There's no obvious death record for her, and it may be that she shunned him after he was imprisoned.

Elizabeth eventually reappeared on the 1901 census, running a coffee house in Grays – an Essex town on the Thames Estuary – with the help of her daughter. At the time coffee houses were enjoying a boom due to the temperance movement, as they offered an alcohol-free meeting place, so Elizabeth was meeting a demand.

Many women were involved in the temperance movement, and it was increasingly linked with women's rights and universal suffrage. They also had a lodger – a coppersmith – living with them. This was particularly respectable, and in a complete contrast to her earlier rather-more-notorious life.

The coffeehouse didn't seem to last though, as when Elizabeth died in 1908 she was resident in Ealing, close to her two sons – who both had large families of their own, and was buried locally.

Her daughter Ellen went on to be an apartment keeper, and never married. Son Charles became a gardener, and died just before the Second World War. Her son Herbert emigrated to Australia and died out there in the late 1940s.

References

Adams, C (1982), *Ordinary Lives*, Virago Press
Daniell, J.J (1894), *The History of Chippenham*, R F Houlston
Devizes and Wiltshire Gazette, 15 September 1870, *Chippenham*
England and Wales: Birth, Marriage and Death Records, held by Ancestry.co.uk
England and Wales: Christening Index 1530-1980, held by Ancestry.co.uk
England & Wales, Criminal Registers, 1791-1892, held by Ancestry.co.uk
Jefferies, S (1987), *A Chippenham Collection*, Chippenham Civic Society
North Wiltshire Herald, 17 September 1870, *Chippenham Chronicle. Concealment of Birth*
UK 1851 census, held by Ancestry.co.uk
UK 1861 census, held by Ancestry.co.uk
UK 1871 census, held by Ancestry.co.uk
UK 1881 census, held by Ancestry.co.uk

UK 1891 census, held by Ancestry.co.uk

UK 1901 census, held by Ancestry.co.uk

UK 1911 census, held by Ancestry.co.uk

UK 1939 register, held by Ancestry.co.uk

Western Daily Press, 27 March 1871, *Somerset Lent Assize, Fifth Day, Saturday. Before Mr Justice Byles*

Wiltshire, England, Church of England Births and Baptisms 1813-1916, held by Ancestry.co.uk

Katherine Abraham or Miller

IN TERMS OF Wiltshire and women's suffrage, the awesome figure
of Edith New (1877-1951) – Swindon-born but London-based –
overshadows much of the grassroots activism in the early 20th century.
The town of Corsham is known to have been very supportive of
the Great Pilgrimage that came through the county in June 1913,
but there are no local names of women that stand out as activists and
speakers, and though the pilgrimage also came through Chippenham
the populace here are thought to have been largely indifferent and
instead responded better to the antis coming through around the same
time. Trowbridge had a branch of the WSPU, with Bessie Gramlick
(or Gramlich) as joint secretary alongside Lillian Dove-Willcox (who
famously evaded the 1911 census by camping out in a caravan on
Salisbury Plain), but not a great deal about their activities has been
recorded. In contrast, the Devizes branch of the WSPU (Women's Social
and Political Union, the group founded by Emmeline Pankhurst and her
daughters in 1903), with secretary Katherine Abraham, appear to have
been much more active.

Katherine was a grocer's daughter, born at Upavon on the edge
of Salisbury Plain at the beginning of 1888. She was the younger of two
children – her brother Edward was two years her senior – and her parents
had married quite late on for the time, which perhaps explains her lack
of other siblings. Her father Joseph had run a grocer's shop on Estcourt
Street in Devizes, probably with the help of her mother Caroline, but by
the time Katherine and Edward were around he'd taken retirement. The
family lived in Upavon for a while, but by the turn of the 20th century
they were back at Estcourt Street where the shop was no longer a going

concern for the family – it appears to have been next door, in a premises that has been occupied by Roses' Hardware since 1947 – but their smart town house was of a good size and they were financially solvent enough to be able to employ a servant.

Katherine's level of education is unknown. She definitely would have attended elementary school – probably at the National School for Girls – and she may have gone further, likely to the Devizes College and High School, as the town's private grammar school was only for boys.

Her father Joseph died in 1902, when she was around 14. The family continued living in the Estcourt Street house, and her brother began to train as a doctor. Katherine was well positioned – unmarried, comfortably off, and probably educated to a good standard – to become involved in the movement for women's suffrage. She became the secretary for the Devizes branch of the WSPU on its establishment in 1911, but had probably been involved in the work of the National Union of Women's Suffrage Societies which had been active in Devizes since around 1909.

There were WSPU members in the area from very early on after that organisation's formation. A member from Bromham wrote to the editor Devizes and Wiltshire Advertiser on the matter of Asquith's promises to parliament in December 1906. And a meeting was organised at Devizes Town Hall in November 1910 where Reverend Geoffrey Ramsey spoke on *The Awakening of Womanhood*, and Wiltshire WSPU members served the tea afterwards. This appears to have been an important point in the formation of the local branch, as – chaired by Miss Mary Beatrice Oldfield of Seend – it represented the coming together of many like-minded souls.

One of the first acts of the Devizes WSPU was to attempt to boycott the 1911 census, in line with other branches nationally. Katherine's mother Caroline wrote her name on their family census form, but this was crossed out later as she did not spend the night of 2nd April 1911 at their house. Instead, Katherine and three other WSPU members – Flora Sainsbury, a domestic science teacher; Evangeline Cross, head teacher of the girls' national school; Kate Allen, head teacher of the national infants' school – hid at an empty house in Victoria Street, Devizes, to evade the census. The enumerators found out, and on 20th April their details were recorded (with various errors – Evangeline was recorded as Eveline) alongside those of Emily Hale, an art teacher who was also away from her lodgings that night to evade the census.

Another known WSPU member, teacher Norah (in actuality Eleanor Hannah) Ussher, may also have been with them on census night, but her father recorded her presence at the family home in Potterne Road regardless. There may well have been others in the Devizes WSPU, who either successfully evaded the census or were recorded by their families even though they were not present. Miss Oldfield of Seend did not boycott the census.

As secretary, Katherine's likely duties would mostly have involved a lot of correspondence. She'd have written to people to arrange meetings, alongside planning the meetings herself. She would have dealt with memberships enquiries and recruitment, and acted on organising resolutions and actions. There would also have been an element of note taking, inviting of guest speakers, booking and selling of tickets, and some fundraising. Other secretaries occasionally wrote to newspapers on suffrage matters, but Katherine does not appear to have done so. It is likely that the meetings that Katherine organised were generally quiet affairs, as none appear to have made the newspapers for unruly conduct – unlike a WSPU meeting at Bradford on Avon town hall in April 1913, where onions and vegetables were thrown at the speakers and threats were made to throw suffragettes in the river.

Katherine, with Norah Ussher and Flora Sainsbury, attended the Women's Coronation Procession through London on 11th June 1911. This was a mass suffragette march, held just before the coronation of King George V, aimed to demand women's suffrage in the new era. Katherine, Norah and Flora – dressed in suffrage colours white, mauve and green – carried the Moonraker banner on behalf of the Devizes WSPU and joined 40,000 others on the route from Westminster to the Albert Hall. Many women dressed as well-known female historical figures, and there were representatives from various different groups and societies in the movement. One of the three women wrote an account of their view of the pilgrimage in the *Wiltshire Telegraph* a couple of weeks later, but it was merely signed 'A Devizes Suffragette'.

There is no obvious record whether the Devizes branch of the WSPU took part in the Great Suffrage Pilgrimage of July 1913. This gathering brought together around 50,000 women along many routes to come together in the name of women's suffrage, culminating in a rally at Hyde Park in London. It was organised by the National Union of Women's Suffrage Societies. The route did not go through Devizes, but did take in nearby Corsham, Chippenham and Calne – so it is possible that Katherine and her fellow members went to watch the women coming through.

It's likely that Katherine stayed involved in the WSPU until their cessation of activities at the outbreak of the First World War. The London branch of the WSPU was involved in recruiting women for munitions work in 1915, but Devizes does not seem to have been involved in this. Katherine married her young man, Jesse – a coal miner from South Wales who had somehow found his way to Devizes – in the autumn of 1915.

Their son Thomas Hayden Miller was born in the October of 1916. At some point that can't quite be pinpointed, Jessie went into the army to fight, and was sent to India. He died out there, as a corporal in the 5th Battalion of the Royal Wiltshire Regiment, at Poona, in September 1918, having contracted influenza that mutated into pneumonia, and was probably a victim of the Spanish Flu pandemic. This left Katherine as a widow with a son aged not-quite-two. She was probably supported by her WSPU friends, none of whom had married, and they encouraged her to take her next steps.

In the spring of 1919, after the war was over, Katherine applied to the war office for funds for a period of training as part of her widow's pension. She got this grant, and moved to the Golders Green area of London with Thomas to train as a Montessori teacher. This child-centred system of education had been popularised in the UK by its founder Maria Montessori a few years earlier, and allowed Katherine to train for a profession alongside caring for her son in the same setting.

Montessori teaching has at the heart of it five key principles: respect for the child, the absorbent mind, sensitive periods, the prepared environment, and auto-education. The idea of auto-education is that the child can self-educate, so teachers, like Katherine, are there as guides rather than instructors, which is a very different system to the strict learning by rote and repeating system that dominated the British education system at that time. Each child therefore respected as an individual, with their own pace of development and way of learning.

Maria Montessori believed that young children's minds – particularly those under the age of six – were like absorbent sponges that took in knowledge from their surroundings without any effort, so Katherine's training would have focused on this principle too. An intense interest in something when concepts can be learned easily – a so-called sensitive period – is also part of the Montessori thinking, as is a prepared classroom designed to facilitate exploration, independence and learning.

After four months of training, Katherine was qualified and able to take up a position. She initially seems to have gone to Bovey Tracey, in Devon, to work, as she was boarding there alongside her son on the 1921 census. Later on, she moved to a position in Sheffield, at a Montessori school headed by Hilda Doncaster – a Quaker and wife of a steel manufacturer. She can be found working there from the late 1920s onwards, and living close to the Sheffield Botanical Gardens.

The Montessori school where she worked was located on Psalter Lane (the building it occupied now houses the city's Interfaith Centre), and in 1931 an advert for the school detailed that they could explain the educational methods at an open day. The same advert also promised a demonstration of Margaret Morris dancing, a method that encouraged grace and good posture, given by Mrs Doncaster's daughter Margaret. Mrs Doncaster had four children, including Christopher, who went on to be a celebrated theatre designer. Katherine's own son Thomas, who came through the same Montessori system, trained as an architect and was practicing by the beginning of the Second World War. Architecture was one of the reserved professions, so he did not have to fight in that conflict.

Thomas, who lived at home with his mother even as a young adult, married during the war years and eventually gave his mother four grandchildren. Katherine appears to have moved back to the London area during the tail end of the war, living in Bermondsey. At this point she would have been in her mid-to-late 50s, and like many of her generation she had not married a second time. She probably continued to work as a Montessori teacher until taking retirement.

Katherine seems to have died in London, at the tail end of 1974. She was 87. But what became of her fellow Devizes WSPU members and 1911 census evaders?

Emily Hale, who was quite a bit older than the rest of her women's suffrage colleagues, later became secretary of The Church League for Women's Suffrage in Devizes, founded in 1913. However, the following year she was placed in Fiddington House asylum in Market Lavington, declared insane, and remained in asylum care until her death in 1937. Norah Ussher had a boyfriend who was killed during the war, and went on to be assistant secretary of the Working Ladies Guild in London. She never married, and died in 1979.

Flora Sainsbury went to Vancouver, Canada, in 1919 to assist her cousin in running a hotel. Later on she was a teacher, then ran a tea-room with her sister who had come out to join her. She was back in Britain before the outbreak of the Second World War, and lived in both Cornwall and Bath before dying in 1955. She had also never married.

Evangeline Cross continued to be headmistress of the Devizes Girls' Elementary School until 1920, then went home to her native Oxfordshire to take up another teaching position, and died there in 1972 aged 98.

Kate Allen remained headmistress at the Devizes Town Infants School until the town's schools reorganised in 1926. After that, she does not appear to have remained in Devizes. She had been suffering from rheumatism of the foot, so may have taken retirement. It is likely that she returned to her native London, and died there in 1935.

References

Adams, C (1982), *Ordinary Lives*, Virago Press

Bexhill-on-Sea Observer, 17 June 1911, *Local suffragists in London protest*

Canada, Ocean Arrivals (Form 30A), 1919-1924, held by Ancestry.co.uk

1921 Census of Canada, held by Ancestry.co.uk

1931 Census of Canada, held by Ancestry.co.uk

Crawford, E (2013) *The Women's Suffrage Movement in Britain and Ireland: A Regional Survey*, Routledge

Devizes County Infant School Log Book, 1908-1926, held by Wiltshire and Swindon History Centre.

Devizes and Wilts Advertiser, 18 December 1902, *Creditors and Debtors, Joseph Thomas Abraham, deceased*

Devizes and Wilts Advertiser, 14 January 1909 *Women Suffrage. Devizes Ladies do not want the Vote – Interesting Debate at Devizes Town Hall*

Devizes and Wilts Advertiser, 8 December 1910 *Correspondence*

Devizes and Wilts Advertiser, 24 April 1913, *Suffragettes mobbed*

Devizes and Wilts Advertiser, 20 February 1913 *The Church League for Women's Suffrage – A Devizes Branch Formed*

England and Wales: Birth, Marriage and Death Records, held by Ancestry.co.uk

England and Wales: Christening Index 1530-1980, held by Ancestry.co.uk

Global, Find a Grave® Index for Burials at Sea and other Select Burial Locations, 1300s-Current, held by Ancestry.co.uk

Hampstead News, 29 January 1914, *Votes for women: Hampstead Women's Social and Political Union*

Marlborough Times, 22 September 1883 *Marriages*

Miller, L (2013) *The Suffragist Pilgrimage: Their March, Our Rights*, WSHC Blog, at https://wshc.org.uk/blog/item/events-mark-centenary-of-suffragist-pilgrimage.html (accessed 25.06.2023)

Sheffield Daily Telegraph, 13 March 1926 *Montessori Class for Children*

Sheffield Daily Telegraph, 9 December 1931 *Montessori*

Sheffield Independent, 28 June 1929 *Teaching that Tells. Montessori School Methods: Sheffield Work*

Simkin, J (1997, updated 2023) *Edith New*, Sparticus Educational, at https://spartacus-educational.com/Edith_New.htm (accessed 25.06.2023)

Simkin, J (1997, updated 2022) *Lillian Dove Willcox*, Sparticus Educational, at https://spartacus-educational.com/WdoveL.htm (accessed 25.06.2023)

The Suffragette, 23 July 1915, *Women's War Service*

Teachers Registration Council Registers, 1914-1948, held by FindMyPast.co.uk

UK 1891 census, held by Ancestry.co.uk

UK 1901 census, held by Ancestry.co.uk

UK 1911 census, held by Ancestry.co.uk

UK 1921 census, held by Findmypast.co.uk

UK 1939 register, held by Ancestry.co.uk

UK, Army Registers of Soldiers' Effects, 1901-1929, held by Ancestry.co.uk

UK, Soldiers Died in the Great War, 1914-1919, held by Ancestry.co.uk

UK, World War I Pension Ledgers and Index Cards, 1914-1923, held by Ancestry.co.uk

Votes for Women, 26 August 1910, *Do not forget*

Whitfield, L (2018), Bessie G's Story, The Women Who Made Me Project, at https://thewomenwhomademe.wordpress.com/2018/03/16/bessie-gs-story/ (accessed 25.06.2023)

Wiltshire Asylum Registers, 1789-1921, held by Findmypast.co.uk

Wiltshire Council teachers' register, held by Wiltshire and Swindon History Centre.

Wiltshire Museum (year unknown), *Norah Ussher*, at https://www.wiltshiremuseum.org.uk/?artwork=norah-ussher (accessed 25.06.2023)

Wiltshire, England, Church of England Births and Baptisms 1813-1916, held by Ancestry.co.uk

Wiltshire Telegraph, 26 November 1910, *Votes for women*

Wiltshire Telegraph, 24 June 1911 *With the Women's Pageant, by a Devizes Suffragette*

Susannah Levitt

S USANNAH LEVITT RAN successful businesses on Chippenham high
street during the 19th century, following fashion and fad to her
best advantage and adapting her career to suit what people needed
and wanted at that time. She called herself Mrs Levitt, despite never
marrying – this would have given her businesses some gravitas as they
appeared to be being run by a widow rather than a spinster, and also
raised an illegitimate daughter at a time when an unmarried woman
giving birth carried a massive stigma. On top of that, in her later
years she ran a boarding house where a young woman concealed a
pregnancy.

She was born in early 1799 in Chippenham, to relatively educated
parents George and Elizabeth (Betty), née Marks. She was the youngest
of their children. Susannah had three older sisters – Martha, Elizabeth
and Mary – and a brother, George, named after his father. There had also
been an earlier brother, also called George, who had died as an infant.
All her siblings except Mary stayed in Chippenham and were active in
the town's trades and life. Mary Levitt, Susannah's next oldest sibling,
married and moved away to Malmesbury.

Susannah's childhood and early adulthood aren't visible in the
records, but it's known she lived in Chippenham during this period. This
is a time when there were no named census records taken, and working
people tend not to appear on official documents, so it's hard to even
know what her father did for a living.

She lost her father when she was 29, however, and he was buried
at St Andrew's Church in the winter of 1828. Her mother then seems to
have gone to Malmesbury to live with Susannah's sister Mary. It's after
this that Susannah's life comes much more into focus.

She makes an appearance in the Pigot's Directory for Chippenham,
published in 1830, as a straw-hat maker. She was one of four women
undertaking this job in Chippenham at that time, and there were two
more – one male and one female – in Corsham.

This isn't millinery, or 'proper' hat making, as for that you might well have had to undertake an apprenticeship and train under someone up-to-seven years in order to call yourself a milliner. This wasn't always the case, but most milliners would have dealt in higher class bonnets and materials other than straw.

Straw, because it was less durable and a cheaper material, was more of an everyday hat for women of all classes, and it's likely that Susannah was good with her fingers and had learnt the skill of plaiting and sewing the stalks together.

The hats that Susannah made were likely a type of Dunstable bonnet, where thick wheat straw was split, and plaited, and the plaits were sewn together. They were extremely common in the country, particularly in the summer, and were often plainly trimmed with a length of ribbon that tied underneath the chin. Fancier examples might have had feathers or flowers included.

Three years after that trade directory was published, Susannah's daughter Emma made her appearance. Her father isn't recorded in her christening record at St Andrew's, and she's just given as 'base born' by the vicar. Whether the father knew of his new daughter or not, he does not appear to have supported Susannah in any way, and she raised Emma alone. Her mother died while living with her sister at Malmesbury, in 1837.

She was still given as a straw-hat maker, alongside five others across Chippenham and Corsham, in the 1842 Pigot's Directory. By this time, fashionable bonnets had started to change shape, heading back

to an earlier type referred to as the cottage bonnet. These had a brim
and crown in a continuous straight line. Susannah's speciality, plaiting
and sewing straw, was still used but usually finer stalks and mixed with
horsehair for textural effects. Larger straw hats were also being made for
gardening and countryside use. These were still very much headwear for
the summer months, however, and heavier and more costly materials
were used in the winter months. This may have meant that Susannah's
work was going through peaks and troughs, and may not have made
enough money to support herself and her seven-year-old daughter.

She appears to have kept it going throughout Emma's childhood
though. She's found in two Kelly's Directories, in 1848 and 1852 as
a straw bonnet maker. Initially she lived on the high street, but then
moved to New Road. Emma grew up and went on to be a day mistress in
a school by the time she was 18.

The transient nature of the straw bonnet business was highly tied
to fashion, so Susannah was bound to keep up with trends. When Emma
married a boot maker in 1855 and moved away to the London area, it
may be that Susannah felt that a change of career was necessary. She
followed another growing fashion and became a tea dealer.

This may have also been due to economic pressures. By this stage,
there was only one straw bonnet maker within Chippenham, a Mrs
Leonora Jones who says she's a straw and Tuscan bonnet maker. Tuscan
straw was imported from Italy, so was high-end fashion. Susannah and
her peers many not have been able to compete. There are also three
milliners and dress makers. In contrast, there are three other tea dealers
in town, but Susannah was the only woman in the business. Someone in
her family had been dealing in tea in Chippenham in the 1820s, but the
full connection to Susannah isn't clear.

Tea had been growing in popularity since the 18th century, and
initially was a fashionable drink for the upper classes and used sparingly.
By the 1830s tea was being drunk by everyone, usually out of china and
porcelain. Huge tea plantations were planted in India and Sri Lanka, as
part of the British Empire, and drinking tea was seen as patriotic since it
supported that empire.

Because the water used to produce tea was boiled, and therefore
did not contain the same impurities as untreated water, it also meant
that tea was a great boon for the general public health. The temperance
movement, which advocated abstaining from alcohol – which had
been a staple drink while water was unclean – latched on to tea as a

perfect alternative. It kept the population sober, straight thinking and industrious, which were all valued by the Victorians.

Therefore, the stage was set for Susannah to make a good living dealing in tea in Chippenham. The product would have come in loose and dried in large tea chests, and been dispensed by the scoop to head for caddies and eventually the teapot.

Susannah, who was by now in her mid-50s, kept this job for several years. She's described as a tea dealer in the 1859 Post Office directory and the 1861 census, alongside other tea dealers in the town.

In 1861 she was living in Foghamshire, and was also taking in boarders to supplement her income. A trade directory of 1865 has her a shopkeeper on Foghamshire, and by 1867 she'd stopped being a tea dealer and focussed on keeping the boarding house. Now in her later 60s, physical housework would have been harder and since she had made enough money to own a house with extra rooms, taking in boarders would have been the obvious way to have an income.

It's as a lodging house keeper that Susannah makes her first and only appearance in the newspapers. It appears that in April 1867 she gave lodgings to a young woman, Sophia Wild, who had been a domestic servant near Reading. It appears that Sophia was around eight months pregnant at that time, but the corset and skirts that most women wore would have gone a long way to hide this from her landlady.

Sophia reported being ill during the night about a month or so later, so Susannah made her some tea. Sophia then made her way to the privy at the bottom of the garden, and returned 10 minutes later feeling better but not saying what had taken place. She spent two days in bed, eventually sending for the doctor who came to examine her.

The doctor figured out what had happened, treated her, and alerted the police. A dead baby girl was found buried in the soil within the privy, who an inquest found could only have lived for around three minutes due to accidental suffocation.

It was decided that Sophia knew of her condition and had made preparations to come to Chippenham from Reading to give birth away from home. However, the case was eventually dismissed and Sophia was not sent to prison.

After this, Susannah left her home in Foghamshire and moved to the town's Springfield Buildings, a handsome stretch of houses in Bath stone which do not run along a main road. She continued being a boarding house keeper until the end of her days.

She died, aged 72, in the January of 1871. Her resting place is St Paul's Church on Malmesbury Road, which was nearer to her house than St Andrew's. She was survived by her daughter Emma, Emma's husband Edward Davis, and five living grandchildren.

References

Adams, C (1982) *Ordinary Lives*, Virago Press
Bath Chronicle and Weekly Gazette, 7 June 1821 *The London Genuine Tea Company*
England and Wales: Birth, Marriage and Death Records, held by Ancestry.co.uk
England and Wales: Christening Index 1530-1980, held by Ancestry.co.uk
Daniell, J.J (1894), *The History of Chippenham*, R F Houlston
Jefferies, S (1987), *A Chippenham Collection*, Chippenham Civic Society
Harrod's Directory of Dorset and Wiltshire (1865)
Kelly's Directory of Wiltshire (1867)
National Portrait Gallery, *Fashion Plates: Headwear - Straw hats and bonnets*, https://www.npg.org.uk/collections/search/portrait-list.php?search=ap&subj=585%3BFashion+Plates%3A+Headwear+-+Straw+hats+and+bonnets&displayNo=60 (accessed 2/7/2023)
Pigot's Directory of Wiltshire (1822, 1830, 1842)
Post Office Directory of Wiltshire (1855, 1859)
Robson's Directory (1839)
UK census collection, held by Ancestry.co.uk
Wiltshire, England, Church of England Births and Baptisms 1813-1916, held by Ancestry.co.uk
Wiltshire, England, Church of England Deaths and Burials, 1813-1916, held by Ancestry.co.uk
Wiltshire, England, Church of England Marriages and Banns, 1754-1916, held by Ancestry.co.uk
Wiltshire, England, Wills and Probate, 1530-1858, held by Ancestry.co.uk
Wiltshire Independent, 30 May 1867, *Concealment of birth*
Wiltshire Times and Trowbridge Advertiser, 22 June 1867, *Chippenham, Alleged Concealment of Birth*

Elise Stein or Grünfeld

I MAGINE BEING INTELLIGENT enough and working hard enough
to achieve a doctorate in mathematics, in an era where women
were only just allowed to earn them, and then being denied the title
by some foreign men because you were a) from a different country
and they weren't sure they recognised the institution you earned your
qualification in, and b) a married woman. This happened to Elise Stein,
née Grünfeld – a well deserving holder of a PhD, but referred to as Mrs
(despite a divorce) when she found work as a maths teacher at Bradford
on Avon's Fitzmaurice Grammar School.

The second daughter of a Czechoslovakian lawyer, Elise was born
in 1903 in Most, a Bohemian city in the northern part of what is now
Czechia. The region was German-speaking – Most's German name is
Brüx – and Elise grew up speaking that language. Her family was Jewish,
well-educated and quite well-to-do.

During the first world war, when the situation for Jews in that area
was good, she and her sister Käthe (four years her senior) attended high
school in their home town, with Elise showing a particular aptitude for
mathematics. She went on to study at the local college at 16, graduating
in 1923, and then went on to the University of Vienna for four further
years – gaining a distinction in maths – and achieving a doctorate in
1928. Her dissertation was titled *Zur Untersuchung von Ebenenkomplexen
in mehrdimesionalen Räumen* (roughly translates as '*For examining plane
complexes in multidimensional spaces*').

Somewhere along the way she'd met and married Ernst, a junior
lawyer in her father's office, in about 1924 and gave birth to a daughter
(Ilse) in 1928. Although both nominally Jewish, Ernst and Elise
considered themselves atheists. However, the marriage did not work out
and ended in divorce in 1935.

After qualifying for her doctorate, and gaining the first part of
a teaching diploma, she had spent eight years as visiting lecturer at
the University of Prague, and then after her divorce moved to be the

Statistical Expert at the Institute of Market Research in Vienna. Her father had died in 1931, but her mother continued to live in Most.

She is known to have travelled to several other countries during the years before the beginning of the second world war. There is a family story that her cousin, Hans, tricked her into ordering tripe – not her favourite food – in various different languages in each of the countries she travelled to.

However, by this point, the situation for Jews in her part of Europe was getting dangerous. Her daughter, then around 10, was excluded from her school in Vienna on the basis of her Jewish background, so she and Elise returned to Prague. Ilse managed to escape in January 1939 as part of the Kindertransport with the help of the Barbican Mission to the Jews, based in London's East End, who saved around 100 children in the nine months up to the outbreak of World War II.

The idea of the mission was that the Jewish children should convert to Christianity, which, since neither Elise nor her ex-husband Ernst were religious, was not a problem for the family. Elise was able to follow Ilse two months later, on a domestic permit – presumably with the idea of being able to care for her – but left her mother and ex-husband behind. A friend, Anna Neithammer, had helped get her a post as a cook in Blackheath, London. Her sister Käthe had married and moved to Chile with her husband, which may have been considered as another avenue of escape, but ultimately the domestic permit provide Elise with the means to leave.

England at the time was not a particularly cosmopolitan place. Many people had not been abroad – the country was decades away from package holidays – and much of the news from the area that Elise came from centred on Hitler and the activities of the Nazi party, so even rescued Czech Jews could be viewed with suspicion. In addition, Elise's doctorate came from a non-British university, so many might doubt the rigour of that education as it was 'different' to that which they had experienced.

Therefore, Elise had to find work in England as and where she could. With the help of people within the Barbican Mission for the Jews she began working as a chamber maid, then a cook and a governess, and the 1939 register – taken a few weeks after the outbreak of the Second World War – has her performing domestic duties for a female accountant in London. This accountant was New Zealand-born Dora Hamlyn, and though the register acknowledges that Elise was a statistics expert, she probably helped Dora as well as doing the cleaning. But on this form her doctorate is not acknowledged. Her daughter Ilse lived separately, initially with the Mission in a home in the Brockley area and then being evacuated to Devon, and Elise's access to her was restricted. Initially they only saw each other at weekends.

In January of 1940, with many of the male teachers starting to be taken into the forces as the war got underway, there were starting to be shortages in teaching staff in many schools. She managed to gain a position as temporary science mistress at Thorn Bank school in Malvern-Wells, Worcestershire. This was a small private school for girls, which did not have a great deal of funds for equipment. Elise taught here on her wits and vast knowledge, as her only scientific equipment was pieces of litmus paper. However, the stability of this job meant that her daughter was returned to her care, and they lived together in Malvern-Wells and later in Carlisle where Elise held a mathematics teaching position for a year from September of 1940 that was slightly better than the previous post but not by much.

From here, she had an interview with the head of The County School (later Fitzmaurice), a grammar school in Bradford on Avon, Wiltshire, on the railway station platform at Derby with a view to replacing his head of maths – Johnny Otter - who was serving in the RAF, and got the job. Whereas the governors of that school were not particularly worldly at that time, the head teacher was young and a Quaker, part of the Rowntree chocolate manufacturing family of York, and as part of the company business had even been abroad.

He recognised that a doctorate from the University of Vienna was equal to one from a British university, and persuaded the governors to take on Elise – though in a nod to their reservations she was still referred to as Mrs and not as Doctor. They may also have had reservations as the previous replacement was also a German Jewish refugee and had been interned in an Enemy Alien camp for a few months in 1940, and they may have feared losing Elise to this fate too – although it was only the men who were interred in the end.

Elise became the senior maths teacher of the school in Bradford on Avon, and her daughter enrolled too. She was well liked by staff and pupils alike, and respected by all. Her heavy accent apparently was difficult to understand at first, but many students found her lessons inspirational. She was paid on the standard scale, with slight deductions for being in a temporary position and technically an alien, but was awarded a special payment for her exceptional qualifications – which they still weren't formally recognising – in 1943.

During this period, both her mother and ex-husband – who had not been able to escape the Nazi regime – were placed by the Third Reich. Communication would have been virtually non-existent, so she probably would not have known of their fate until after the war. Her mother was sent to the Theresienstadt Jewish ghetto, with other Czech Jews, which eventually became a labour camp. She was then sent on to Auschwitz, where she died in the gas chambers sometime in either 1943 or 1944. Ernst, Elise's ex-husband, was sent to the ghetto at Łódź, Poland, where he died of starvation in 1943. Elise's teaching position, and life in the UK, must have included the hope that her family and friends had somehow survived.

Elise remained at the grammar school in Bradford on Avon until the end of the school year in 1945, when – the war having ended in May, at least in Europe – it was expected that the head of maths would return from RAF duty and take his place again at the school. In practice, this did not happen until 1946, and another German Jewish refugee was employed until then. The job did belong to the original head of maths, Johnny Otter, but it is fair to say that Elise was far better qualified for the role than he was.

She moved to be maths teacher at the Greenford County School, in Middlesex, and her daughter moved with her. After a few years here she was able to make the switch back into working in higher education in London, ultimately at Brunel University. She was active in both the English and German language fields of maths, and here reclaimed the title of Dr again as it was finally recognised. She was elected a member of the London Mathematical Society on 17th November 1949, and eventually became a British citizen.

Her daughter lived with her in Wembley, also working in higher education, until her marriage in the late 1950s, after which Elise appears to have lived alone. She visited her sister Käthe in Chile in the late 1950s and early 60s. After Käthe's husband's death in the early 1970s Käthe went back to Germany and lived in Munich, so Elise had a ready-made base there when she travelled for work. She eventually had two grandsons.

She also continued her research while working in higher education. There is a picture of her attending the Edinburgh Mathematical Society

Colloquium in St Andrews, Scotland, in 1976. She is also mentioned as a member of the Austrian Mathematics Association by the International Mathematical News published in Vienna in 1977. By this point she was living in Latymer Court in Hammersmith, built in 1934 and described at that time as the largest single luxury block of flats in Europe.

In 1978 she was awarded a Golden Doctorate from the University of Vienna, an accolade given to those who have reached 50 years since their original doctorate and are still continuing to research and push the boundaries of their subject. She still did not stop there – in 1983, at the age of 80, she delivered a paper in Germany on '*The practical treatment of stress concentrations and singularities within the finite element displacement algorithms*', and there is mention of her having delivered lectures for the Open University.

She died in 1991, aged 88, and was buried close to home in London. Her daughter, Ilse Ryder, died in 2023.

References

1939 England and Wales Register, held by Ancestry.co.uk

Association of Jewish Refugees – *Ilse Ryder*, on https://www.ajrrefugeevoices. org.uk/RefugeeVoices/Ilse-Ryder (accessed 18.6.2023)

BBC Radio 4 *Home Truths*, on https://www.bbc.co.uk/radio4/ hometruths/0241ilse.shtml (accessed 18.6.2023)

Berry, K (1998), *Bradford on Avon's Schools: The Story of Education in a Small Wiltshire Town*. Ex Libris.

EMS 1976 Colloquium, *Colloquium photo* (1976), on https://mathshistory.st-andrews.ac.uk/EMS/photo_1976/ (accessed 18.6.2023)

England & Wales, Civil Registration Death Index, 1916-2007, held by Ancestry. co.uk

Grünfeld Family Genealogy, (accessed 18.6.2023) https://freepages.rootsweb. com/~prohel/genealogy/names/grunfeld/grunfeld1.html

Guardian, The, (Monday 3 April 2023), *Ilse Ryder Obituary*, on https://www. theguardian.com/education/2023/apr/03/ilse-ryder-obituary (accessed 18.6.2023)

London Mathematical Society Newsletter, The (June 1991), *Elise Stein*

Mathematics Genealogy Project (accessed 18.6.2023) https://www.genealogy. math.ndsu.nodak.edu/id.php?id=105938

Ody, V (2005), *The St Laurence Story*. Ex Libris.

Österreichische Mathematische Gesellshaft (edited) *International Mathematical News 117* (Nov 1977), Wein

Rio de Janeiro, Brazil, Immigration Cards, 1900-1965, held by Ancestry.co.uk

Russ, S. B. (1980), *The mathematical works of Bernard Bolzano published between 1804 and 1817*. PhD thesis The Open University.

Staff register book of The County School, Bradford on Avon, held by Wiltshire and Swindon History Centre

Stein, E. (1985). *The practical treatment of stress concentrations and singularities within finite element displacement algorithms*. In: Grisvard, P., Wendland, W.L., Whiteman, J.R. (eds) Singularities and Constructive Methods for Their Treatment. Lecture Notes in Mathematics, vol 1121. Springer, Berlin, Heidelberg. https://doi.org/10.1007/BFb0076276

Union of Czech Mathematicians and Physicists (1935) *Zpráv Y O Druhém Sjezdu Matematiků Zemí Slovanských Praha, 23.-28. Září 1934*

Sister Josephine

U NLIKE HER FAMOUS SONG namesake immortalised by folk singer
Jake Thackray, Sister Josephine did not establish a pontoon team
in her convent nor sit with her boots up on the altar screen. Instead,
she was one of the first sisters from the English mission of the Sisters of
Joseph of Annecy in the Wiltshire market town of Devizes, and went on
to lead a prominent convent in both Chippenham and Malmesbury, and
eventually a well-respected school in Newport, South Wales. But a holy
life and fulfilling her God's work did not mean that everyone respected
her choices, and at one point she was stoned for her efforts.

She'd been born as Elizabeth (Josephine was a name she took
later on in life, when she dedicated herself to the convent), in Loughrea,
County Galway in Ireland in 1838. She was born a few years before the
famine, which hit rural Ireland hard in 1845, and she had a sister – Maria
– born three years later. It's unknown exactly what her father Jeremiah
did, but he appears to have moved the family into Galway city at some
point during the next few years, probably due to the famine, as a land tax
record finds him living in a small house there in 1857.

Therefore, the family did not leave Ireland during the famine, but
arrived at some point later as its effects continued to be felt. Her parents
either did not survive long over in England, or remained in Ireland, and
left Sister Josephine alone to educate her sister. She was placed in a
convent. Maria later joined the Sisters of Charity.

Sister Josephine moved to Chippenham in Wiltshire. As Elizabeth
Toomey she was the first godmother mentioned in the baptisms of the
original St Mary's Church in St Mary's Place, Chippenham, which start in
1857. The church was founded in August 1855, and operated as a catholic
school where Sister Josephine – at this point still called Elizabeth –
taught. It was there that she must have first met Father Larive, the first
missionary of St Francis de Sales to work in England. The original rather
plain church is now used as the modern-day church hall, a new building
having been established in the early 20th century on Station Hill.

Eliza, the wife of prominent Chippenham attorney Thomas Abdy Fellowes, was an early Catholic baptism at St Mary's. The family lived at Langley Lodge, perpendicular to Langley Road in Chippenham. Eliza was the daughter of Frederick Rooke of Lackham House, and had been baptised and married in the Church of England, but things were slowly beginning to change during the 1850s and 60s. Several of her daughters followed her into the Catholic faith.

The first UK census to feature Sister Josephine is the 1861. She had left Chippenham to become a teacher, and found a place at a convent school on Bath Road in Birmingham. Aged 22, she had gained the position of assistant school mistress, and was in charge of various teenage girls being educated at the convent.

Sister Josephine, having worked and lived in a convent for several years, decided to take the veil herself. She had been recommended by Father Larive. She went to the founding convent in Annecy, France, and became a novice in the congregation in September 1863. It was from there, in August of 1864, that the English mission of the Sisters of St Joseph of Annecy was founded. Two Sisters – Sr Athanase (sometimes Antoinette) Novel, who was originally French, and Sr Stanislaus Bryan, who was of Irish extraction but had grown up with the sisters in India – travelled from the congregation's Indian mission in Kamptee (part of modern-day Nagpur) by ox cart to the coastal port of Yanam and thence on to France, in order to found the English mission.

The impetus for founding the mission came from a British Army officer, Captain Dewell, who had seen the good work of the sisters in India and asked them to come to his home country of Wiltshire. Since Sister Josephine had already been teaching in Chippenham, about ten miles away from the intended site in Devizes, she was perhaps the obvious choice to accompany Sisters Athanase and Stanislaus on their endeavour. They travelled across Europe to Devizes, took up residence in the town's Wyndham Villas – a former priests' residence by the Kennet and Avon Canal – and it was here that Josephine took the veil on 22 November 1865.

The ceremony was performed by Hon. Rev. Dr. Clifford, Bishop of Clifton. Newspapers of the day reported that the ceremony had not been seen in Wiltshire since the episcopate of Francis Mallet, the last Roman Catholic Bishop of Salisbury, in 1558. Alongside a postulant, Miss Sarah Smith, Elizabeth Toomey (described as 'a novice of several years' standing') became a nun professed. Her hair was cut, and she was divested of the vanity of worldly dress, and made vows of poverty, chastity and obedience. She became Sister Mary Josephine, but was always known as Sister Josephine.

In the run up to this, and as part of the convent foundation, the three Sisters had established a poor school in Monday Market Street, in a rented warehouse. It was then that the trouble started. Despite the fact that the school, and the mission, were founded with the best of intentions, educated poor children for just a penny a week and gave out clothing to those in dire need, the three nuns were met with suspicion by the Devizes population. The struggles between Protestantism and Catholicism in the UK were nothing new at this point in the 19th century, and Devizes was no different though perhaps more vociferously anti-Rome than most. Catholicism was starting to gain a foothold in England again after the Irish famine of the 1840s and the arrival of many destitute people in need of work. The moralising tone of the educated middle and upper classes, which was reported in the newspapers of the day, implies that the destitute Irish were an underclass and therefore somehow a scourge on the land and were bringing their unsavoury religion with them. And they were taking local jobs too.

A speaker at a Devizes function at the time warned of the new nuns, saying of the 'necessity of avoiding the follies of Catholicism and of shunning the nuns who dappled (sic) in witchcraft.' The *Devizes and Wiltshire Gazette* scathingly reported on the 'opening' (inverted commas theirs) of the Catholic Church in 1865, describing it as plain and ugly, and that the nuns were, with one exception, foreigners. Feeling continued to run high, and in 1866 1,600 people in Devizes attended a talk on the evils of Catholicism, and how convents should be ended. Such was the hostility the three sisters – Josephine, Athanase and Stanislaus – were even stoned by local residents as they went about their work.

A series of lectures by the Devizes and North Wiltshire Protestant Association in the autumn of 1866 probably didn't help with integration into the town. At one, Lieutenant-Colonel Brockman of London advised the Devizes protestants to 'Pull down the rookery and drive the rooks out of the town!', 'rooks' being a derogatory term for Catholics. He also spoke against convents, and said that 'every female who frequented the confessional was degraded to the level of the lowest prostitute who walked the streets.' Despite Protestantism being deeply upheld in Devizes, this turned the meeting into an uproar.

Even in the face of this, Sister Josephine and the others persevered. They opened a school for middle- and upper-class children in Wyndham Villas, in addition to their work with the poor children, and walked the ten miles to Chippenham every Sunday to Sister Josephine's original church, to teach the Catechism and play harmonium for mass. They also undertook work in Westbury, several miles to the south of Devizes.

In 1866, however, the Sisters of St Joseph of Annecy opened a new convent and school in Chippenham's Marshfield Road, and needed a mother superior. Sister Josephine came back to Chippenham from Devizes and took over that role. Situated in Suffolk Villas, apparently at 11 and 12 that road, the 1871 census has her with two female scholars, neither of whom were born locally, and two other nuns, running the convent and the education of the school, and providing space for a religious visitor to live. Stanislaus and Athanase remained in Devizes.

There does not appear to have been the local opposition to the establishment of the convent in Chippenham that was experienced in Devizes. There are no reports of witchcraft or stones being thrown. It is probable that the establishment of St Mary's in the 1850s probably paved the way, and the townspeople – less isolated due to the mainline railway and the Great Western Road - were more accepting of the Catholics and foreigners. However, newspapers of the time have virtually nothing about Catholic activities in the town, so it's likely that much of Josephine's activity flew under the radar.

Ten years later, however, on the 1881 census, the convent did not have any pupils, and perhaps could not be called a school in the

strictest sense of the word. Josephine was still mother superior, with
four other nuns serving in the institution, and they had three other
women boarders or visitors. Convents would often house Catholic
widows as they were trying to get back on their feet after their husband's
death, and St Joseph's Convent in Chippenham was clearly no exception.
The convent would have offered a calm and serene atmosphere, with a
structured timetable and considerable prayer.

The lack of pupils probably played a part in the ending of the
Chippenham convent in 1884, when the community moved to a house
made available by Captain Dewell in Malmesbury – about six miles to the
north of Chippenham but still in Wiltshire. There was no further convent
in Chippenham until the 1930s, when St Margaret's established on
Rowden Hill.

There had been a foundation in Malmesbury since 1867, when
Father Larive had left Devizes to establish a base there. Sister Josephine,
after her period as mother superior in Chippenham, also took on this
role in Malmesbury. In 1891 there were four other nuns besides her, in
addition to several boarders and three domestic staff – meaning that
Sister Josephine could devote herself to more spiritual matters than
running a household. This would have been a new way to devote her to
Jesus.

By 1897 Sister Josephine had crossed the River Severn, and was
established as mother superior at the Stow Hill Convent and School
in Newport, South Wales. This establishment had been founded from
Devizes in 1873 (using money from the dowry of Sister Mary Joseph,
who had been educated there), and Mother Athanase had gone from
there to be the first mother superior taking most of her community
with her. Only two sisters and a postulant were then left in Devizes,
Westbury's work ended in 1875, and the focus of the Sisters of St Joseph
of Annecy became this new school and convent in Newport. By 1901 her
companion Mother Athanase was getting on in years, and was no longer
mother superior, leaving the UK for the Sisters' base in Annecy, where
she spent her dotage. Sister Josephine, at this point in her early 60s,
became mother superior in Newport.

The Newport school was a huge undertaking. Sister Josephine
had 14 teachers underneath her, teaching art, music, needlework,
French, German and basic elementary subjects like reading, writing
and arithmetic. The census returns for 1901 and 1911 show there was a
full complement of domestic staff – including ladies' maids – boarding

pupils aged between 12 and 17, and a host of young women in their early twenties who are referred to on the census as resident students but were probably novices in training to become nuns. There was even a resident artist. Many of the teachers, like Sister Josephine, were Irish-born, but the cooks were both French. The students, in contrast, were mostly drawn from the local area – except one who was born in India.

This convent and school appears to have thrived. Sister Josephine was still mother superior in 1911, but by now in her early 70s she had taken a step backwards from the day-to-day life of the school. Her jurisdiction was over the novitiates and teachers, of which there were many, but only five boarding pupils were in her household. The convent and school, however, spread over four houses, and with many teachers employed most pupils would have attended just in the daytime. The school and convent eventually outgrew its premises in the 1940s, and was moved to Llantarnam Abbey a few miles north.

Sister Josephine, as she was starting to age and lose her sight, went on to be mother superior at a much smaller community in Wincanton in 1912, and then on to a boarding school in Clifton, Bristol. She then moved back to the Newport convent to be a part of that community again, and served as a councillor in the town. She is on the 1921 census at that convent, given as the retired superior.

She lived to be 97, and in her last years was cared for by her community at the convent. She died in 1933, and is buried in Newport. The last of the Sisters of St Joseph of Annecy left Devizes in March 2021, during the Covid-19 pandemic, and joined the community in Newport.

References

Bridport, Beaminster, and Lyme Regis Telegram, 30 November 1865 *Taking the veil*

Catholic Times and Catholic Opinion, 20 October 1916 *Convent of the Sisters of St. Joseph, Stow Hill, Newport, Mon, Boarding School for Young Ladies*

Devizes and Wiltshire Gazette, 26 January 1865 *Opening of a Roman Catholic Church in Devizes*

Devizes and Wiltshire Gazette, 11 October 1866, *Uproar at the protestant meeting*

Devizes and Wiltshire Gazette, 25 October 1866 *Protestant Lectures in Devizes*

Devizes and Wiltshire Gazette, 25 March 1869, *Died*

Devizes and Wilts Advertiser, 7 September 1876, *St Joseph's Place, Devizes*

Devizes Heritage, St. Joseph's Roman Catholic Primary School Devizes. At http://www.devizesheritage.co.uk/St_JosephRCSchool.html (accessed 26 November 2023)

England and Wales: Birth, Marriage and Death Records, held by Ancestry.co.uk

England and Wales: Christening Index 1530-1980, held by Ancestry.co.uk

England and Wales: 1921 census, held by Findmypast.co.uk

Ireland, Catholic Parish Registers, 1655-1915, held by Ancestry.co.uk

Ireland, Griffith's Valuation, 1847-1864, held by Ancestry.co.uk

Ireland, Valuation Records, 1824-1856, held by Ancestry.co.uk

Jefferies, S (1987), *A Chippenham Collection*, Chippenham Civic Society

Sister Josephine, https://jakethackray.com/lyrics-and-tabs/sister-josephine/ (accessed 26 November 2023)

Sister Josephine Twomey Necrology, privately provided by Ann Rutter of Sisters of Joseph of Annecy

Sisters of Saint Joseph of Annecy *Farewell to Devizes*, at https://srsofstjosephofannecy.org/index.php/en/england/201-farewell-to-devizes (accessed 26 November 2023)

St. Joseph's Convent, Newport, Mon. at https://www.newportpast.com/gallery/photos/php/photo_page.php?search=tredegar%20house&search2=yyyyyy&pos=5 (accessed 26 November 2023)

St Mary's Church, Chippenham, records, held by Wiltshire and Swindon History Centre

Swindon Advertiser and North Wilts Chronicle, 29 June 1868 *Devizes: Taking the veil*

Taking stock: Catholic Churches of England and Wales. Devizes – Immaculate Conception. https://taking-stock.org.uk/building/devizes-immaculate-conception/ (accessed 26 November 2023)

UK census collection, held by Ancestry.co.uk

Weekly Register and Catholic Standard, 2 November 1867, *Convent of St Joseph, Devizes.*

Western Daily Press, 30 January 1865, *New Catholic Church at Devizes*

Wiltshire, England, Church of England Births and Baptisms, 1813-1922, held by Ancestry.co.uk

Wilts and Gloucestershire Standard, 25 August 1855 *Chippenham*

Wilts and Gloucestershire Standard, 25 November 1865 *Taking the veil*

Amelia Gueriott or Green

S INCE SHE HAD ancestry from expelled French protestants, the
Huguenots, who were known to have incredible skills as cloth
artisans, it comes as no surprise that it was the silk industry that,
indirectly, brought Amelia Gueriott to Malmesbury.

Rather than obtaining work at Avon Mills, however, like many
generations of the town's women and girls have done, she instead
arrived in the town via her brother-in-law's appointment as manager of
those mills in the 1850s. But, instead of throwing silk thread, like her
Huguenot ancestors had done for centuries before her, Amelia instead
opted to work with the poorest in the town and took a position as the
schoolmistress at the workhouse. Later on, she married a gardener
and raised a family. But, in her fifties, she suffered from debilitating
depression that the doctors at the time attributed to the perimenopause
– something completely treatable today - and spent her declining years
locked up in an asylum at the mercies of Victorian mental health care.

She'd been born in August 1836 in Shepton Mallet in Somerset,
where her silk thrower father Louis Gueriott had taken her family
from London in 1830. He was clearly of Huguenot stock – his name,
profession and London birthplace point to French origins - but since he
appears to have been an illegitimate birth (his married mother had an
affair which resulted in his existence) in late 1799 it is hard to work out
exactly when his ancestors arrived in Britain.

Huguenots, French protestants who were not permitted to
worship their way in their own country, started to arrive on these shores
in the later 1600s and into the 18th century. Where Louis', and therefore
Amelia's, ancestors came from and arrived is open to question, but with
an obviously French surname he may have been able to trade on the
Huguenot reputation for fine cloth artisanship, even if his connection to
it was a little distant. Huguenots were known in 17th century France for
producing high quality taffeta, velvet, ribbon, brocades, and silver and
gold cloth, and their reputation travelled with them.

Amelia was the youngest of several children, and their names speak of both their French origins and non-conformist religious roots. Her eldest three siblings, Eliza, Louise Marie, and Josiah, were born in London. Then the move to Shepton Mallet occurred, as Louis and Amelia's mother Elizabeth had Frederick there in 1830, Elizabeth in 1832 and Louis Joseph in 1835. Like her brother Frederick, Amelia was baptised in the Wesleyan Methodists Church in Shepton Mallet in 1836, but several of her siblings were christened in the Church of England. Her sisters Elizabeth and Louise Marie died young, when Amelia was five and six respectively.

Amelia's father worked as a silk throwster in the small silk industry around Shepton Mallet. This was an industrial process where the skeins of silk are cleaned, twisted and wound onto bobbins, and would have been an important part of making the thread strong enough to weave with. As the 19th century wore on, throwsters would have operated machinery that did this in the mills, but Louis likely knew how to do this by hand process. The throwsters at the Malmesbury silk mills would have treated the silk in the same way.

However, the 1841 census, taken when Amelia was five, finds the family on Garston Street in Shepton Mallet, with her father claiming to be a tea dealer rather than working in the silk industry. Whether this was accurate or not is open to question, as a dealer in tea would have had more social standing than the labouring and silk throwing that Louis was previously doing in London, and it would have been a step up the job ladder. He's also not listed as a tea dealer in a Shepton Mallet trade directory published two years before this, as the only one listed is Benjamin Ellis on the town's high street. He's also not in the list in a trade directory published a year after the 1841 census. The tea dealing could therefore be particularly short lived on Amelia's father's part, or wishful thinking. But more money and social standing may have enabled Amelia to achieve a better education than her siblings, as she was educated until at least the age of 14, while many of them were working by the age of 9. Her siblings were labourers, sleeve binders, errand boys and silk throwsters themselves.

In 1848, when Amelia was 12, her mother died. This was reportedly of an infected cat bite to the hand, which would have festered and been untreatable without the anti-biotics we rely upon today. By the time of the 1851 census, her father was back being a silk throwster, while one brother wove velvet in one of Shepton Mallet's cloth production facilities and another worked as a carpenter and joiner.

Her sister Eliza married Walter Butt in 1850, and moved away to the home counties for a time with his job as a press man in the silk mill at Rookey, near Watford. Amelia would have remained at home with her father, and as the only daughter much of the housework would probably have fallen to her.

At some point between 1853 and 1855, her brother-in-law Walter Butt brought his family to Wiltshire when he was appointed manager of Malmesbury Silk Mills which imported raw silk from China, mostly for ribbon weaving. Amelia – who had recently gained a stepmother, Betsy – came up from her childhood home to stay with her sister Eliza on the High Street, and chose to settle. The Butts were perhaps not the first managers of the revived Malmesbury silk industry, which began again in 1852 in the 1790s-built mill buildings on St John's Bridge. However, they were almost certainly the second in that position, appointed by new owner Mr Lewis, and Amelia's arrival in Malmesbury would have been in the later part of that decade as she is known to have accepted a schoolmistress job at the workhouse in October 1860.

Under the Poor Law Amendment Act of 1834, which had brought in a new national system of poor relief and established Poor Law Unions and boards of guardians for them, workhouses had to provide schooling for at least three hours a day for the children they housed. Malmesbury workhouse, built on Sherston Lane in 1837-8, was no different, and Amelia was employed alongside a schoolmaster, Abel Richmond – who would have taught the boys while she had the girls – to fill this provision.

Much of Amelia's instruction of the children would have been on the three Rs – reading, writing, arithmetic – and Christian scripture and values. This would have included dictation, and learning times tables by rote. Another part of her job would have been to prepare the girls for working in domestic service, as this was their most likely source of employment, and to train them to be useful, industrious and virtuous. The boys would have had more education in correct grammar, history and geography, while Amelia held classes in needlework and knitting.

In addition to this, as school mistress Amelia had to keep the children clean and tidy, accompany them when they left the workhouse for a walk or to attend church, and help the master and matron of the institution with discipline and sub-ordination. Workhouse inmates were often reminded that their situation meant that they were the lowest of the low, and they were supposed to show proper respect for their betters.

In 1861, when Amelia appears on the census at the workhouse, she had 47 girls listed as scholars in her care. They were aged between two and 16, so it may be that the older girls gave Amelia some help with the younger. The workhouse master and matron, at this time John Thomas Sinkin and his wife Catherine, would have overseen the care provided by Amelia and her counterpart schoolmaster Abel Richmond.

Amelia's qualifications for the job would have been assessed on a grading scale that assessed her competence and running of her classes under the remit of the Committee of Council on Education. At the lower end of the scale she would have had to be able to read fluently, write a little, do simple mathematics, and know some details about the life of Jesus. These skills were built upon up the scale, until the top qualifications included detailed knowledge of scripture, correct and accurate dictation, details of grammar and prose, complicated arithmetic and – usually for the men – geography (particularly of the British Empire, and Palestine) and an outline of British history. Amelia and Abel's work could have been viewed by inspectors at any time.

Amelia stayed in her job at the workhouse until 1867, by which point the Master and Matron – John Thomas and Catherine Sinkins – and their sons seem to have left the union. Malmesbury was comparatively to others a small workhouse, and many Master and Matron couples seem to have started their careers there and after a few years moved on to bigger pastures, as there are different people in post on every census. The Sinkins were no different, and upped sticks to Eton Union Workhouse.

The leaving of the Sinkins may have been one reason for the ending of Amelia's job. Another reason was her marriage. She married John Green, a gardener employed by various big houses at Burton Hill, in April 1867 at the church where she'd been baptised in Shepton Mallet. Couples often returned to the bride's home parish to marry. Her brother Louis Joseph, who was based in London, married on the same day at the town's independent chapel. The marriages were reported in several newspapers, indicating the social standing of the family in the area at this time.

Elsewhere in her family life, her brother Louis Joseph was established as a carpenter and joiner in London. Her brother Frederick, who worked as a butcher, had gone out to Australia but died shortly after arriving in 1858. Her other brother Josiah had gone to Cardiff, and found work as a labourer. Oldest sister Eliza and family stayed in

Malmesbury past the change in ownership of the town silk mill in 1869, but eventually followed the new silk business to its base in Derby and lived the rest of their lives there.

Amelia and John had six children together: Frederick William at the tail end of 1867 (who may have been on the way before his parents married); James Walter in late 1868; John Henry who was born and died in 1870; Henry John in 1872; only daughter Lucy Ellen in 1874; and finally Frank Richard in 1876. Both the 1871 and 1881 census returns see Amelia's family growing in Malmesbury, with her husband John bringing in an income from his gardening work, and Amelia typically credited as a married woman with no occupation – but in reality, busy with the children, the cooking, the clothing, the laundry, the cleaning, and many other unpaid tasks that were deemed not important enough to be mentioned by the census takers. Losing a tiny baby, as she did with John Henry in 1870, was typical for the period, with a high rate of infant mortality that had no respect for class or occupation. They also lost their youngest son, Frank, at the age of eight in 1884.

Round about 1886, however, the picture of Amelia's family life starts to become less rosy. At about the age of 50 she had her first documented bout of mental illness. This was later described as melancholia, brought upon by 'change in life' according to her doctors. Today the link between the changing hormones caused by perimenopause and bouts of depression and low mood is acknowledged and treated – with hormone replacement and with anti-depressant medication. Back then, the doctors knew that depression or 'melancholia'

was linked to the change, but would not have had the medical knowledge to describe it. Nor know how to treat it effectively. Instead, patients were recommended rest and relaxation, and special diets – believing that a more robust body would result in a more robust mind. Some doctors recommended administering alcohol.

Amelia's initial illness seems to have resolved itself with gentle care, but by 1890 she was suffering more lengthy and severe symptoms, so was admitted to the County Lunatic Asylum in Devizes. She was still there at the time the 1891 census was taken in April of that year. Amelia was 53 and was described as a lunatic. Her former schoolmistress profession had been attributed to her in the records, so was still held in high enough esteem for her previous work in the workhouse.

After this care she was declared cured, so was sent home to her family – husband John and daughter Lucy were there to look after her. However, the causes of Amelia's illness did not seem to settle down, and she suffered another bout of melancholia and depression from December 1893. Her husband John tried to cope, but eventually admitted defeat and she was dispatched back to the asylum with a letter from him in February 1894.

'I am deeply grieved that I have been obliged to send my poor wife back to the asylum,' says John's letter. He and their daughter had got into the habit of leaving small portions of food around their house in the hope that Amelia would find them and eat them, as she would not sit at the dining table with them.

The doctors' report on this admission, from the asylum casebook, explains their diagnosis and Amelia's symptoms:

Recurrent melancholia. She is very low and depressed, reticent and emotional. Refuses food. Says she has no right to it. Refusal to remain at home as she thought it was not hers and she had no right there. Is very deluded and cannot be reasoned with.

Taciturn, depressed and melancholic. Though husband and daughter are kind to her and her home is comfortable, says she has no home and that she ought not to stop at home. Her husband states that at times he has great difficulty in keeping his wife in the house – seems to get away clandestinely saying that she must not stay at home, and yesterday she became very violent and unmanageable and he was obliged to seek assistance to control her.

It appear that by this stage Amelia's condition was incorporating severe self-esteem issues as well as crippling depression. Whether this could have been relieved by modern medicine and talking therapy is a matter for today's doctors, but neither were an option in 1894 so she was submitted to the treatments available. She was placed in the asylum for safety, looked after and fed well. But her mental issues were not addressed. The asylum noted she was well nourished, but had a weaker heart. The case book also said she'd had a good education, but reports her as suicidal. This verdict may have been born from her reluctance to engage in the world around her.

Doctor James Wilson reported very little change in Amelia after her admission, though she was put on an extra diet and gained a little weight. She wanted to leave but clearly wasn't well enough. She was put onto a continuous admission to the asylum in 1895, and never went home again.

The early reports on Amelia in the asylum were that she sat apart from other patients and averted conversations. They felt that she acted as if she was suspicious of everyone. It was also reported that she was prone to fainting due to heart weakness. Her mental health issues were clearly deeply seated by this time, and no attempts to treat them were recorded in the case book. The care she received simply seemed to revolve around the hope that she might one day get better.

That day did not come. A report from the Amelia's case book from 22 January 1898, four years after her admission, says:

> She is very miserable and depressed, speaks in a low tone of voice, never enters into any continuous conversation. Evidently very introspective and sits broodingly over her sewing most of the day. Never brightens up in the least degree. Very pale and in feeble health. Has fainting attacks at times due to cardiac weakness.

Things did not improve for Amelia as the years went by. By 1903 there is a report of her having auditory hallucinations, and talking to herself. She was described as dull, vacant and depressed in September 1906.

At this point, with no improvement and no active care to speak of, it was clear that Amelia was going to be in the asylum until the end of her life. That came in April 1907, over 13 years after being admitted to the county asylum, when she succumbed to dysentery after being ill for a week. She was 71 years old.

Her daughter Lucy sent a letter a week after her mother's death thanking the doctors and the asylum for taking care of her 'dear mother'. Lucy married a year later, having also been working as a school mistress.

References

Athelstan Museum, *Malmesbury Silk Mills*, at https://www.athelstanmuseum. org.uk/malmesbury-history/architecture/malmesbury-silk-mills/ (accessed 27.8.2023)

Crowley, D A, (1991), *The Victoria History of the County of Wiltshire Volume XIV: Malmesbury Hundred*. Oxford University Press

England & Wales, National Probate Calendar (Index of Wills and Administrations), 1858-1995, held by Ancestry.co.uk

England & Wales, Non-Conformist and Non-Parochial Registers, 1567-1936, held by Ancestry.co.uk

Higginbotham, P (2003) *The Workhouse: The story of an institution...* at https:// www.workhouses.org.uk/education/workhouse.shtml, at https://www. workhouses.org.uk/Malmesbury/, at https://www.workhouses.org.uk/ admin/index.shtml#teacher (accessed 27.8.2023)

Historic England (1951) *Avon Mills, Inner Buildings*, at https://historicengland. org.uk/listing/the-list/list-entry/1269278?section=official-list-entry (accessed 27.8.2023)

Jansson, Å. (2021). *Diagnosing Melancholia in the Victorian Asylum*. In: From Melancholia to Depression. Mental Health in Historical Perspective. Palgrave Macmillan, Cham.

London, England, Church of England Baptisms, Marriages and Burials, 1538-1812, held by Ancestry.co.uk

London, England, Births and Baptisms, 1813-1906, held by Ancestry.co.uk

Matthews, M (2017) *A Cure for Melancholy: Victorian Medical Advice on Treating Depression*, at https://www.mimimatthews.com/2017/04/03/a-cure-for-melancholy-victorian-medical-advice-on-treating-depression/ (accessed 27.8.2023)

NHS Inform (2022) *Menopause and your mental wellbeing*, at https://www. nhsinform.scot/healthy-living/womens-health/later-years-around-50-years-and-over/menopause-and-post-menopause-health/menopause-and-your-mental-wellbeing (accessed 27.8.2023)

Pigot's Directory of Somerset (1842), held by Ancestry.co.uk

Robson's Directory of Somerset (1839), held by Ancestry.co.uk

UK, Lunacy Patients Admission Registers, 1846-1921, held by Ancestry.co.uk

UK Census Collection, held by Ancestry.co.uk

Warner, F (1921) *The silk industry of the United Kingdom. Its origin and development*, Dranes

Weston-super-Mare Gazette, and General Advertiser, Saturday 27 April 1867, *Births, marriages and deaths*

Wiltshire County Asylum Case Book, held at Wiltshire and Swindon History
     Centre
Wiltshire County Asylum Patient Register, held at Wiltshire and Swindon
     History Centre
Wiltshire, England, Church of England Births and Baptisms, 1813-1922, held by
     Ancestry.co.uk

Isabella Langhorne or Edridge

I SABELLA MARIA CONSTANTIA Langhorne, named after her mother (and also perhaps for her father's fascination with Italy and its people), was orphaned by the time she was three. Her mother Isabella, the second wife of her clergyman-and-poet father John Langhorne, had died giving birth to her in 1776, and her father then died in 1779, aged only 45.

She had a half-brother, John Theodosius Langhorne, who was eight years her senior, but he had been brought up by an aunt since his own mother's death in childbirth, so the orphaned toddler Isabella was alone in the world. She'd been born in Blagdon, Somerset, where her father had been the Reverend since 1766, but he'd really made a name for himself while working for several churches in London – and it was there that Isabella was sent.

Her father had become friendly, while living in London, with the Gillman family. Thomas Gillman, who was involved in the law (although what sort of position he held is not clear), his wife Catherine and their daughter Catherina Elizabeta were named Isabella's guardians and protectors in her father's will.

She was removed from Blagdon to their house in Great Ormond Street – at this stage a street of important people living in smart sizable town houses that dated from the beginning of that century and not the site of a famous hospital for sick children (it wasn't built until 1852) – and began a life in London as their ward.

The Gillman's daughter and only child Catherina Elizabeta was in her later teens, so the age gap between the two girls was vast, and it seems likely that they all lavished their attention on the young Isabella, who would have been brought up in considerable privilege for the time.

This was a great time to be a privileged child, as the period brought in huge amounts of books, toys and games aimed at children, and began to value and educate their developing minds in a far more structured way. Isabella's father had instructed that she would benefit from the sale of his goods and chattels to help fund her life with the Gillmans, all her mother's clothes, and a further sum of £1,000 to be held in trust for her when she reached the age of 21. He also bequeathed her and her brother a diamond ring apiece.

When Catherina married in February 1783, Isabella was around the age of seven. Though Thomas Gillman was still in Great Ormond Street, Isabella went with Catherina to be the ward child in her new marriage.

Catherina had married Esmead Edridge, the lord of the manor at Monkton House, in Chippenham – down the Great Western Road from London. The Edridge family, who were initially Quakers and had mostly been born in Bristol, had owned the large house since at least the 1740s.

At this stage, Esmead was the eldest living son, but there were many other siblings still associated with the house – his older sister Love Mary had recently married and moved to Bath, but younger brothers Thomas, John and Abraham were all unmarried and at the house, running a business as clothiers of the town. A clothier was someone who had cloth produced for them in workshops that they owned, and concentrated on the buying and selling of that material.

In addition to the four men, their widowed mother Love and unmarried sister Martha completed the large household that Catherina and Isabella joined.

Though the original Monkton House had a great deal of space for the large family, shortly after the marriage, Esmead had Monkton House renovated. This altered what had originally been a substantial farmhouse-style property into a grand Georgian mansion of many rooms.

He appears to have made a reasonable living as a merchant, as well as being Lord of the Manor, but it may be that Catherina's dowry brought in additional funds for the building project. His brother Abraham Lloyd Edridge had a smaller house – River House - built in a similar style, possibly using the same architect and builders, in St Mary Street just across the river. The property is today used as apartments, and has purpose-built sheltered accommodation on the land leading down to the river that may initially have been used for fulling and dyeing cloth.

Isabella, at just seven, now grew up in this great house full of people. Esmead and Catherina, who had no children of their own, considered her their daughter to all intents and purposes and treated her as such. They educated her, probably at home with a governess, and she was included as part of the wider Edridge family. There were no other children known to have lived at Monkton House at the time.

This position changed in 1798, when Isabella had just turned 22 and had come into her inheritance. She engaged in a clandestine marriage with Abraham Lloyd Edridge, Esmead's younger brother, who had been in the position of uncle to her throughout her childhood. Catherina and Esmead were said later to have been deeply offended by this act because of this prior relationship. They married by license, meaning that banns did not have to be read publicly, and the marriage may well have come as a bit of a surprise to more than just the Edridge family.

Abraham, a clothier and occasional soldier, was a good 15 years older than Isabella, and had converted from his original Quaker faith to the Church of England in 1791. He had also fathered an illegitimate child – John – when he was in his late 20s. This John, despite his illegitimate birth, was regarded as his heir, and technically became Isabella's stepson. The couple never had any children of their own.

As an aside, Esmead and Abraham's brother Thomas also seems to have had an illegitimate son at around the same time, but in contrast he was not acknowledged. John's elevation appears to have been due to a lack of any legitimate male heir anywhere in the family.

Isabella then went to live with Abraham, probably at River House on St Mary Street and became mistress of that property. They are known to have paid hair powder tax around now, so would have been fashionable enough to wear wigs. Isabella's marriage technically made her the social equal of Catherina and other gentry wives, but given the controversy surrounding the marriage it is unclear whether they were accepted in local society.

In the very early 1800s, Catherina – who was then in her early 50s – started to suffer mental health issues and in the parlance of the time was declared a 'lunatic'. Descriptions of some of her behaviour, from the newspapers, put this as close to what we would modernly describe as dementia.

She was removed from Monkton House to Fisher House, which appears to have been a London residence for the mentally ill. As her ipso-facto daughter, Isabella tried to work with the family to help Catherina be placed in environments that were comfortable, going through legal means if necessary.

Around the same time, Isabella and Abraham moved from Chippenham to Pockeridge House, on the edge of Corsham, which is now on Ministry of Defence land and was converted to an officers' mess during the second world war. The property there was substantial, and Abraham's son John lived with them there when he wasn't serving with the Royal Navy. In this house she was able to be a gentry wife away from the house she'd grown up in, but still maintained her links with Chippenham.

Esmead, her adoptive father, died in 1812. At this stage Isabella's care of Catherina seems to step up a gear, perhaps as he was not there to stand in the way. She went through legal means to have access to Catherina despite the judgement of lunacy (and the considerable societal stigma associated with it), and arranged with brother-in-law Thomas - Esmead's heir - for her to have her own room and an increased financial allowance.

This made the newspapers, and the scandal over Isabella's marriage was raked over by the press. It was agreed, however, that Isabella could take Catherina out for drives in her carriage, and could look after her at Monkton House for periods of time as she was more comfortable there and her symptoms reduced. Isabella argued that since Catherina had looked after her from childhood, it was now time for her to look after her guardian.

Catherina, despite her illness, managed to outlast Isabella by six years. Isabella died at Pockeridge in 1820, aged 44, and seems to have been buried close to where she'd grown up in Chippenham, at the town's St Andrew's Church.

Catherina died in 1826, and was buried with Esmead and Isabella at Chippenham. Abraham continued to live at Pockeridge, with his son John and John's first two wives (there were three in all), and died in Bath in 1842. He is not buried with Isabella.

ISABELLA MARIA
CONSTANTIA EDRIDGE,
wife of
ABRAHAM LLOYD EDRIDGE
of Pockeredge in the County of Wilts
died March 28th 1820
Aged 44 Years.

References

Adams, C (1982) *Ordinary Lives*, Virago Press

Bath Chronicle and Weekly Gazette, 15 March 1798

Bristol Mercury, 10 September 1842, *'Births, Marriages and Deaths'*

Bristol, England, Non-Conformist Baptism, Marriage and Burial Registers, 1644-1981, held by Ancestry.co.uk

Cumberland Pacquet, and Ware's Whitehaven Advertiser, 20 August 1788, *Books*

Daniell, J.J (1894), *The History of Chippenham*, R F Houlston

Devizes and Wilts Advertiser, 20 October 1898, *North Aisle*

England and Wales: Birth, Marriage and Death Records, held by Ancestry.co.uk

England and Wales: Christening Index 1530-1980, held by Ancestry.co.uk

England & Wales, Prerogative Court of Canterbury Wills, 1384-1858, held by Ancestry.co.uk

England & Wales, Quaker Birth, Marriage, and Death Registers, 1578-1837, held by Ancestry.co.uk

Jefferies, S (1987), *A Chippenham Collection*, Chippenham Civic Society

Oxford Journal, 10 April 1779, *On Thursday last...*

Oxford Journal, 1 April 1820, *Births, marriages and deaths*

Morning Chronicle, 20 August 1813, *Law Intelligence. Court of Chancery. August 19 1813. Lunatic Petition. Exparte Eldridge in the matter of Eldridge.*

Morning Chronicle, 8 February 1814, *Lunacy. Ex Parte Edridge, Ex Parte King, in the matter of Edridge.*

Morning Chronicle, 9 February 1814, *Court of Chancery, February 8, Lunacy. Ex Parte Edridge, Ex Parte King, in the matter of Edridge.*

Newcastle Chronicle, 19 January 1771, *Plutarch's Lives*

Public Ledger and Daily Advertiser, 25 May 1814, *Law Intelligence. Court of Chancery. Ex Parte Edridge, in the Lunacy of Edridge.*

Salisbury and Winchester Journal, 3 April 1820, *Salisbury, Monday April 3, 1820*

Somerset, England, Church of England Baptisms, Marriages and burials, 1531-1821, held by Ancestry.co.uk

Statesman (London), 24 August 1813, *Lunatic petition*

UK census collection, held by Ancestry.co.uk

UK, Poll Books and Electoral Registers, 1538-1893, held by Ancestry.co.uk

Wiltshire, England, Church of England Births and Baptisms 1813-1916, held by Ancestry.co.uk

Wiltshire, England, Church of England Deaths and Burials, 1813-1916, held by Ancestry.co.uk

Wiltshire, England, Church of England Marriages and Banns, 1754-1916, held by Ancestry.co.uk

Thermuthis, Emily and Lucy Ashe

S OME SIBLINGS LUCKILY share a tight sisterly bond, others are as
different as night and day – and while they love each other and share
a background, other values like politics can vastly differ within family
members of the same generation. And this is equally true for those
born of a privileged background as well as those from more modest
beginnings.

Thermuthis and Lucy were sisters who exemplified this difference
between siblings. Alongside middle sister Emily, they were the three
daughters of Squire Reverend Robert Martyn Ashe of Langley Burrell
at the tail end of the 1850s. They had a comfortable upbringing for the
time, and a great deal of money and influence behind them. But where
Thermuthis followed the typical politics and activities of landed gentry
at the time, and Emily married and followed the more-expected path for
women of this era, Lucy turned her back 180 degrees on this lifestyle and
instead worked tirelessly with the poor and underprivileged to make the
world a better place.

All three sisters make brief appearances in Robert Francis
Kilvert's diaries of the 1870s (they were published as *Kilvert's Diary,
1870–1879* around the time of the Second World War), as Squire Ashe

was part of the landed gentry circles that Kilvert moved in at that time – and the sisters were Kilvert's second cousins via his mother. Kilvert mentions dining at Langley House, their home, on several occasions during the diary, and there is a detailed description of Thermuthis and Emily in his writings.

Thermuthis Ashe was the eldest sister, born in 1856. Sometimes known as Mutie or Thersie, she was her parents' second-born child, but her older brother – named Robert after his father – had died a year earlier of whooping cough and convulsions aged about 18 months. The next sister – Emily Ashe, known to the family as Syddy or Syddie – followed in 1857, and then Lucy Ashe was born in 1859. There were no further children, and no boy to inherit the house and title, so Thermuthis became heir apparent until such time as she married, as under the law at the time a husband would assume the wife's property.

The three sisters would have enjoyed the best of country life growing up at that time, going into the nearby market town at Chippenham for anything that they needed, as Langley Burrell where they lived was a small village.

Both the 1861 and 1871 censuses find the family at home in Langley Burrell with eight servants in residence – in the early years the girls would have had a nursemaid, and later on a governess, and the house had a housekeeper, a cook and various other domestic maids. Their father, who though a reverend who could technically be in charge of the local St Peter's Church, concentrated mostly on the running of the parish and passed the church over to Francis Kilvert's father. He was also a magistrate and justice of the peace in Chippenham.

A newspaper report of the time says that Robert Ashe suffered some ill health and spent time abroad in better climates. Thermuthis, Emily, Lucy and their mother would also have played a great part in the parish life growing up, and the sisters by the standards of the day would have been expected to grow up into genteel young ladies and marry well, probably from among the local gentry. Their father apparently did not approve of mixed dancing, or even mixed tennis for his daughters, so it is likely that their contact with young men was limited.

Kilvert described Thermuthis, known as Thersie, on a visit to their house with two of his sisters in January of 1871, when she would have been around fifteen.

25 January 1871

A fly took Fanny, Dora and myself to dinner at Langley House at 7.30.
The Ashes were very agreeable and Thersie Ashe was in the drawing room
before dinner sitting on an ottoman in a white dress, white boots and
gloves, almost a grown-up young lady and looking exceedingly nice with
her long dark hair and brilliant colour.

Kilvert's gaze also fell upon Emily Ashe towards the end of that
year, when she was around fourteen:

Wednesday 27 December 1871

After dinner I went with Dora to call at the John Knights' at the farm
on the common. At the cross roads we met Mrs Ashe with Thersie and
Syddy going round to the cottages giving the invitations to the New
Year's supper at Langley House. Syddy is magnificent entirely, splendidly
handsome. I never thought her so beautiful before. Her violet eyes, her
scarlet lips, the luxuriance of her rich chestnut curling hair, indescribable.
She is said by my mother to be very like her great grandmother, especially
in her chestnut curling hair.

Syddy's great grandmother, and indeed that of Thermuthis and
Lucy too, was Thermuthis Martyn, who had married a former Reverend
Robert Ashe of Langley Burrell in 1775. Kilvert's diary also makes
mention of Emily being in 'agonies of grief' at the death of Emperor
Napoleon III in 1873, and being miffed that she'd not seen the 13th
Hussars when they trooped through Wiltshire on their way to Colchester.
Youngest sister Lucy does not appear to have been mentioned at all, at
least not in the published portion of Kilvert's diaries, and was perhaps at
this stage too young to have been worth much notice.

Lucy's journals, which began in August 1874 when she was around
15, hold an account of the sisters' childhood. That summer all three girls
holidayed, as usual, in a hotel in Clifton, Bristol, in the charge of their
governess and aunt, and spent time roaming the downs with a family
named the Priestleys. The following summer they also holidayed with the
Priestleys, but this time further down the coast at Portishead, and then
back to Clifton. Lucy was encouraged with her art and sketching, and
often filled the front pages of her journals with drawings.

The journal from 1878 gives more of their countryside childhood
as it must have been, as though Lucy had now reached the age of 18, she

was still very much considered a child in the eyes of the household. In this period, when being a teenager wasn't really a thing, childhood was considered to last until well into the late teens, and this must have been the case for both Thermuthis and Emily too. Lucy's journal also lists interactions with neighbours and friends who were part of their daily pattern of life.

Tuesday 25 June 1878
Read to Papa till 12. Then went and swam my boat in the little stream at the bottom of the field. Momsie came there with me in the afternoon and he is making a weir at one end. I have made a harbour at the other end and a duck pond, and put my ducks, fish and boat there.

Wednesday 26 June 1878
I went to my stream in the morning then went in and read to Papa. Captain Ashe, Walter and Lulu came to us for lunch and stayed until after five. Walter and Lulu played with us at the Dell all the time.

Thursday 27 June 1878
Read to Papa till 12 then went and swam my boats and fed chicks and doves. Ditto in the afternoon. ...

Friday 16 August 1878
Went to the drawing class in the morning. Mary and Priscilla Awdry and Mary Strong came back to lunch with us. Pilly in the carriage with us. We walked about the fields in the afternoon then we had a spelling bee. Then the Awdrys went, and we made pancakes. We got the stuff ready early to get light by teatime then we played the French game. I went to read to Papa but came down in time to toss the pancakes. After tea we had a ball which lasted till Mary went at nearly 9.

Lucy's 1879 journal recounts more of the same, including a fancy party at Hartham Park – just outside Corsham – when the weather was 'hopelessly wet', and she spent most of her time in the summer house with Mrs Goldney and the Misses Dickson. There was also a trip to Bath to have her photograph taken.

Their mother died at the end of 1884 – when the sisters were around 27, 26 and 24 – and their father a month later in January 1885, supposedly of a broken heart following his wife's death but in practice probably of a more definable medical reason.

Thermuthis then inherited the house, and became the landowner, and Emily and Lucy lived at the house with her just as before. Despite

being of eminently marriageable ages, and even verging into the realms
of being left on the shelf in the parlance of the time, none of them
showed any inclination of marrying for a good while. Their finances
would have consisted of their family inheritance, income from tenants
on their lands, and dividends from some investments.

Lucy's 1886 journal recounts a trip to Italy that May, where
they went by train to Lake Como, then Lucerne and into the Alps.
And her account of February 1889 talks of attending a butter-making
competition with Emily.

Monday 18 February 1889

Siddie and I went in early to the butter competition. Siddie was drawn
for an afternoon competition but we stayed all morning and looked on.
I went for lunch at the Keary's and Siddie at the Riches. The others came
in in the afternoon after the butter was finished. We went to the room
upstairs and Lady Neeld gave away ten prizes. Siddie was commended
and got a certificate. A great many people were there.

Emily's skill with the butter churn holds a hint of her life to
come, as it is around this point that the sisters' lives really began to take
different directions. Their family closeness remained, but each had an
entirely different path.

Emily married Edward Scott, a one-time soldier but now decidedly
a landed farmer, in 1891 at the Langley Burrell church.

Lucy described her sister's wedding day as 'so strange, almost like a
dream', and recounted that 'Siddie looked lovely, everyone said so. There
were eight bridesmaids, Mutie (Thermuthis) walked first with Maud
Scott, then I and Rhoda Prodyers, Rich and a Long, Francie and Sybil.
Werdon carried her train. He looked very nice in his naval uniform. The
church looked very pretty.'

Emily took up her own jobs as a farmer's wife on Edward's land
in Kent, which was a large farm near Hawkhurst. They eventually had
four children: Gladys – who became a mountaineer and a member of the
Ladies Alpine Club – and sons Robert, Charles and Arthur (known as
Noel). Although they farmed in Kent, they were frequent visitors to the
family home in Langley Burrell. One son, Robert, was killed in the first
world war. Her youngest son, Noel, took up farming like his father. Emily
died in Kent in 1926, while her husband Edward lasted until 1931.

In contrast, neither Thermuthis nor Lucy ever married.

Thermuthis, as lady of the manor, assumed various duties of public life. She was deeply involved in village affairs, donating and supporting the poor and needy within the community, and a supporter of the village church that had been in her family for generations. A family story is that the matter of her marriage was considered, and that Lord Methuen of Corsham Court was in the frame – so they went for a turn about the garden together to see if they would suit. It was decided that they wouldn't, and the matter was dropped. Clearly extremely religious, like both her sisters and many of her family, she acted as a church warden, and one of the few female wardens in the diocese in the early 20th century (it was part of the wider Bristol diocese), attending the diocesan conference regularly. She also served on the ruri-decanal conference, an event concerning rural parishes.

Langley House remained a focal point for the community under her tenure as it was during her father's day. The extensive grounds were used for political meetings, village and church fêtes – there are mentions of her having entered gardening competition categories at various fêtes and produce shows in the newspapers of the time. Her other chief hobby was archery, and she was often seen practicing this in the grounds of the house, right up until several months before her death. At her demise she was one of the oldest members known of the Society of Wiltshire Archers. She was also a member of the local Beaufort Hunt, but did not actually ride with them – instead providing land for the practice.

Politically, she was a staunch Conservative, perhaps typically for a landowner of her background, and was head of the local Women's Conservative Association. Lord Londonderry – a cousin of Winston Churchill – once addressed a political meeting at her residence. She gradually sold off pieces of land that she had inherited – she'd owned West Kennet Manor through a connection of her great grandmother, but sold it in 1921. She also owned a local patch of woodland – Bird's Marsh – and various extensive parcels of land via the church holdings that extended down into Chippenham itself, as part of what is now the town was a section of Langley Burrell Within parish. Several of these were sold off in the later years of her life, and her name is now remembered on streets created on the land itself – so Ashfield Road, Ashe Crescent and Ashe Close stand as memorials.

Thermuthis Ashe died in 1935 after a short illness, aged 78. She is buried at St Peter's Church in Langley Burrell. Her will made provision for her four Maltese terriers for as long as they lived.

Lucy Ashe seems to have continued living at Langley House with Thermuthis through much of the 1890s, still involved in village life and matters. There were visits abroad and to Emily and family in Kent. However, in a 180° turn around in the very late part of this decade, she turned away from the Conservative and landowning lifestyle of Thermuthis and the established family, and instead moved away to live in London and perform social work among deprived communities.

She was staring her 40th birthday in the face, and this may have been a catalyst for making a change. Family recount that she had intended only to stay in London for a week or so, but ended up staying for more than forty years. Her journal for the summer of 1899 has her beginning social work in Clerkenwell for a few days at a time, before returning home to more usual matters of attending parties and running the Sunday School.

She was visiting Emily and her family in Kent on the 1901 census, with no profession given, but ten years later she was resident at the Twentieth Century Club in Notting Hill. She apparently said 'I throw in my lot with yours. I stay among you.' when she experienced life in Southwark, and did so wholeheartedly.

This residence was a ladies club, founded in 1902, which had 105 bedrooms and was there for the purpose 'to provide furnished residential rooms and board at economical prices, for educated women workers engaged in professional, educational, literary, secretarial or other similar work.' It's likely that Lucy moved into that club early in its life, and at one point she referred to it as the 'New Century', which may have been an older name for it.

Her 1904 journal details the sorts of cases and work that she was involved in, and indicates that she was one of several other unmarried women carrying out the same sort of tasks – which is probably the pool of available workers that early social work had to draw from. Women, particularly those from this class background and means, were often thought to embody the caring nature that those from deprived communities needed in order to progress.

Tuesday 26 January 1904

Went to London to the COS. I heard I am elected member of the Thrift Sub Committee at the Central. Miss Lendrum is ill, Miss Joyce is taking her place. She offered to give me the keys but I refused. Took one case after the Committee Meeting. Out of work, also brother and sister.

Mother a deserted wife and in provident family had earned £3 till recently never saved. Visit cases of underfed children for Victory Place School & Joseph. Open air treatment for daughter. Has a laundry.

Wednesday 27 January 1904

Finished school enquiries. Took 3 cases, Clarke and a failure pension, Walters stock for charity, and a nice widow want my work. Visited Dan who wants to be a COS agent, and Miss Caldwell, a failure machinist who won't give references.

...

Thursday 4 February 1904

2 cases. McDonald, a drunken out of work, and Mrs Kidman, a nice old woman for a pension. Miss Benedict, Miss Chapman, Miss Crawford, Miss Western, and Miss Joyce there, and Miss Dodd came at tea time. Mrs Toynbee for a short time & was quickly consulted over cases. I had the thrift committee and took one out of two of the cases at the other committee. A great many working men there.

Lucy's profession on the 1911 census was given as a Honorary Secretary of a Charity Organisation living on private means, which fits the remit of the 20th Century Club. While she lived there, she had income from another London property and presumably some inheritance to live on which initially gave her means to survive while working, but within a short time she largely financed her own work. Sometimes this involved selling her original paintings. One of her sketch books gives an account of being on a fortnight's holiday in Switzerland when the First World War was declared.

She was probably at the 20th Century Club on the 1921 census too, as she appears on the electoral registers for that year, but the official return for that part of the residence does not have any names included. The club had ceased to exist by 1924, but Lucy remained living in their buildings until at least 1932, so it may be that another organisation had taken the premises over.

She kept an office at 3 Doddington Grove in Southwark, and is remembered as a particularly dedicated and tireless worker, regularly putting in unpaid 18-hour days for the benefit of the borough's poorest residents. Southwark of the time was known for being a place of poor housing and tough living, with parts regularly flooded by the Thames and families crammed into one room in back-to-back accommodation and sharing one toilet with several neighbours. A large drive was underway to remove the slums and replace them with better quality housing – this was a big part of Lloyd George's Liberal government – and Lucy joined this effort.

At the beginning of the First World War she concentrated on helping the families of the borough who had their main breadwinner serving overseas – so focusing on mothers and children in the most part. This work led to being made the first Chairman of the Child Welfare Committee in 1919. She was also on the very first Pensions Committee in the early 1920s and – in direct contrast to her sister Thermuthis – was elected as a Labour Party member of Southwark Council. In later years she served as an Alderman for Southwark. Her work passions also included the health of residents, particularly around the care of people who had contracted tuberculosis.

She later had a small office in Steedman Street from where she offered advice and help to the people she represented and served, and would paint and sell pictures to finance the help she was able to give. Hundreds of people benefitted from her work, and knew her as 'the lady with the satchel'.

She was only persuaded to leave Southwark and the people and streets she loved at the height of the Second World War blitz, with bombs regularly falling into the nearby roads. Six people took over the work that she had done alone. At this time she was into her 80s, and her health was beginning to suffer after all the years of hard work. Some residents thought she had succumbed to a bomb, but in reality she moved home to Langley House in Wiltshire – which at this time was owned by Emily's son Major Charles Scott-Ashe – for the duration.

Her office in Steedman Street was bombed, as were many other places in the borough. After the war, she was remembered by a block of flats bearing her name in Peacock Street.

Her health was not good enough for her to return after the war, and she lived quietly at Langley Burrell for the rest of her life. She died in 1949, on her 90th birthday, and was remembered later that year with a memorial in the grounds of St Peter's Church, and a great niece was named after her. In her will she left £150 to the Southwark Labour Party. A primary school now sits on the site of the block of flats in Peacock Street.

Emily's line, via youngest son Noel as his older brother Charles never married, inherited Langley House and the estate. Subsequent generations, though originally named Scott, have added the hyphenated

Ashe to their surnames as an inheritance condition. The estate was sold in 1998.

References

Ashe, L. *Collected journals 1874-1904*. Private collection

Bristol Mercury, 24 May 1856, *Births*

Bristol Times and Mirror, 20 December 1884, *Death of Mrs Ashe*

Bristol Times and Mirror, 21 August 1897, *Langley Burrell: Bazaar*

British History Online, *Parishes: Avebury*, at https://www.british-history.ac.uk/vch/wilts/vol12/pp86-105 (accessed 17.1.2024)

Census 1921 of England and Wales, held by Findmypast.co.uk

Clifton Society, 27 August 1891, *Marriages*

Crawford, E. (1999) *The Women's Suffrage Movement: A Reference Guide 1866-1928* Routledge

Daily News (London), 8 December 1921, *Robbing pockets of the poor*

Devizes and Wilts Advertiser, 18 October 1877, *Chippenham: The Hurricane*

Devizes and Wiltshire Gazette, 2 November 1905, *Wiltshire: County Notes*

England & Wales, National Probate Calendar (Index of Wills and Administrations), 1858-1995, held by Ancestry.co.uk

Fagence, M. (1949) *Lucy The Crusader Had Way With Her*, in *Daily Herald*, Tuesday 29 March 1949

Kelly's Handbook to the Titled, Landed & Official Classes for 1909 (1909), *Ashe, Miss Thermuthis Mary*, Kelly's Directories, London

Kilvert, R.F. (1870-9) *Kilvert's Diary, 1870-79* (Penguin)

London, England, Electoral Registers, 1832-1965, held by Ancestry.co.uk

North Wilts Herald, 1 February 1935, *Langley Burrell's Loss*

Reading Mercury, 31 January 1885, *Deaths*

South London Observer, 14 January 1949, *Obituary: Southwark Social Worker*

South London Observer, 11 February 1949 *Disappointed*

South London Observer, 29 July 1949 *Isaac's prize goes to striking docker*

Southwark and Bermondsey Recorder, 15 December 1922, *Feeding of necessitous children*

Southwark and Bermondsey Recorder, 17 February 1928, *Central Southwark Labour Party*

Southwark News, 2 March 2017, *Looking back at the slums of Southwark*

The Spectator, 17 May 1856, *Births*

UK Census collection, held by Ancestry.co.uk

Vote, 9 November 1928, *Women borough councillors*

Walford, E (1919), The County Families of the United Kingdom *Ashe, Miss, of Langley House, Wilts* Robert Hardwick

Western Daily Press, 26 January 1935, *Death of Miss T. M. Ashe*

Wiltshire, England, Church of England Births and Baptisms, 1813-1922, held by Ancestry.co.uk

Wiltshire Telegraph, 19 January 1889, *Nominations of candidates*

Wiltshire Times and Trowbridge Advertiser, 5 January 1895, *Cottagers and their rates*

Wiltshire Times and Trowbridge Advertiser, 12 August 1933, *Fruits and vegetables*

Wiltshire Times and Trowbridge Advertiser, 2 February 1935, *Langley Burrell: Death of Miss Ashe*

Wiltshire Times, 15 January 1949, *Miss Lucy Ashe*

Wiltshire Times, 8 October 1949, *Langley Burrell: Memorial unveiled*

Harriet Wigmore and Mary Ann Salter

ABORTION WAS ILLEGAL in the UK until 1967, so unfortunately when we hear about it publicly before this date it is likely because it has gone disastrously wrong. This is the case in Harriet Wigmore and Mary Ann Salter's story from 1883, which may also feature elements of injustice in the British legal system of the time. It's up to the reader to decide based on the evidence.

Wherever your politics, moral and religious beliefs take you on the subject of abortion, a crisis pregnancy is exactly that – one that a woman feels that she cannot continue with, whether for health, mental health, society factors, or any other myriad of reasons. And until a woman faces that situation, it is a real unknown as to how she will react and then choose to act. In most countries around the world abortion has been illegal at some point – and in some it still is, or is verging on being again – and therefore making a choice to end a pregnancy puts a woman into a particularly murky place morally, religiously and societally. But wherever you personally fall on these matters, some women will still want abortions.

Abortion is, therefore, very much part of women's history. Particularly in an era when 'good' girls were supposed to be chaste until marriage, sexual desire on the part of women was barely even known about, much less discussed, and illegitimate children carried a huge societal stigma. However, men who did engage in sexual intercourse outside marriage – although perhaps frowned upon – were not subject to the same stigma, and male desire was an acknowledged concept throughout all walks of life.

Therefore, when Mary Ann Salter – a single Wiltshire woman not in her first flush of youth – realised she was pregnant in the spring of 1883, she had to decide whether to keep the baby and face the wrath of society, or undergo an illegal abortion.

She'd been born in Chippenham in 1850, the oldest of nine children of Joseph Salter - gardener and haulier and his wife Ann. The family lived in a small cottage in The Butts, to the east of the town. After some schooling she lived at home with her parents and siblings, and contributed to the family income as a dressmaker. However, unmarried and staring her thirties in the face, she left the confines of a Wiltshire market town and went up to London, gaining a position as a cook in an affluent townhouse in Chester Place, Marylebone. She was there for six years. She worked for a chemist, John Maitland and his family, as one of several servants with the family. Her employer had several unmarried sons living at home and working in his business, and the house had various young men also living there while working as John Maitland's assistants in the business or studying medicine.

It's unknown exactly who fathered Mary Ann's child, it could have been one of her employers' sons or one of the students or assistants, or someone else entirely, but during the spring of 1883 she lost her job and returned home to Chippenham, to her recently widowed mother's care. About this time she began to complain of 'indigestion'.

Most women at this time were kept ignorant of the mechanics of sexual intercourse until they were married – when it was therefore considered necessary for them to know – but even then information (usually lying back and thinking of England) was not passed on easily between mother and daughter, and men were often ignorant too. The attitude of many doctors was that women had no sexual feelings apart from the urge to have children. So, it may be that Mary Ann did not know exactly what had happened to her.

Her lover may also have been uninformed to a degree – unmarried men were often not given the full picture either, and contraceptives at this time were very much in their infancy. There were leather condoms for men, but these were expensive and had to be asked for directly at the chemists as they weren't displayed. Women could use an inserted piece of sponge on a string that was coated with a spermicide substance, but only if they knew about it, which Mary Ann probably didn't.

Therefore, when Mary Ann complained of indigestion, her mother took her on the train to see a herbalist in Calne, the next town over, for a remedy as this would have been cheaper than seeing a doctor.

This herbalist was Harriet Wigmore, née Powell, who at this time was in her early 40s. She'd been born in about 1840, on the border of Radnorshire and Herefordshire. She had married her husband Isaac in 1866 in Wolverhampton, and they'd had six children together. Isaac, who was born around Charlton Park, had come back to Wiltshire to run a pub

at Lea near Malmesbury, possibly the Foresters Arms, making Harriet a
landlady for a time. By the early 1880s he was settled in on Lickhill Road
in Calne as a gardener and Harriet ran a herbalism business alongside
him. She had, only a month before this case began, stated in court that
she was a certificated midwife too.

On Mary Ann's first visit to Harriet, she was supplied with some
liquid and 16 powders to take to cure her indigestion. This, obviously,
didn't work, and Mary Ann made several subsequent visits for further
treatments, accompanied on occasion by relatives and friends of her
mother. Whether the true nature of Mary Ann's condition became
obvious to Harriet during these visits is unknown. Harriet insisted,
later, that she did not know at all, and certainly outwardly she was still
treating Mary Ann for digestion-based complaints.

Since Mary Ann was still not cured and had taken to her bed,
Harriet came to visit her in Chippenham, and they spent some time
alone talking. Mary Ann then, four days later, went again to visit Harriet
in Calne. Upon her return she felt unwell, vomited, and went to bed.
Then a further three days later Harriet again came to see Mary Ann and
her mother, and this time – according to witnesses – made it clear that
something had happened to Mary Ann. Her mother stated that Harriet
had said: 'If anyone asks what is the matter you say it is a tumour, but it
has burst now, and she will soon be all right.' And another witness said
that she'd said it was a bloody tumour and she would soon be all right
and up in two or three days. These witnesses also say that Harriet took
something away in her basket. The following day a doctor was called, who
said that Mary Ann was suffering from inflammation of the womb and
peritonitis, and sadly Mary Ann died later that day – 16 June 1883.

Given the now serious nature of the matter, a post-mortem was
performed on her the following day by the doctor. The opinion was that
she had died either from the effects of the noxious drugs (fennel and rue
were found), from the effects of an instrument used upon her, or from
both. Harriet was subsequently arrested.

Information about how to administer an abortion was well known
in whispers among married women at this time, for occasions when
they felt they could not afford another mouth to feed. Some doctors
at the time reckoned that one in four pregnancies ended this way.
There were many dangerous methods: pints of gin, hot baths, knitting
needles inserted into the womb, falling downstairs. Alternatively, there
were dangerous drugs, which brought on an abortion as a side-effect:

adhesive plasters contained diachylon, which was made from lead and could be bought from the chemist, and would then be eaten. There was also a mixture called 'hickey-pickey' or 'hiera picra', which was bitter apple, bitter aloes and white lead, which could all be purchased from the chemist. Infusions of rue were a known irritant, and had abortifacient properties, and was sometimes combined with other herbal infusions to increase potency.

It is likely that at least two of these methods – inserting an instrument, and a rue and fennel infusion – were used in Mary Ann's case. But whether they were administered by Harriet the herbalist – as the subsequent murder court case claimed - or by Mary Ann's mother and friends, is open to question.

At the court case, on 6 July 1883, the prosecution alleged that Mary Ann's mother claimed Harriet said to her that she had 'instruments', but they were never to be seen. Harriet apparently carried away something from the house in a bag. And the post-mortem, having found no trace of any noxious drugs in Mary Ann's stomach, concluded that the cause of death was the instrument used to expel the pregnancy, which was used with enough force to cause the internal bruises and that Mary Ann could not have administered that herself. This was the case against Harriet.

Her defence argued that Harriet had not been seen to possess one single noxious drug in this case, and that a single piece of 'rue' might not actually be the plant. And that the instruments described were not to be seen, much less obviously used. They also felt that the day the instruments were used was the day that Mary Ann had travelled to Calne and back on the train, and that if she'd suffered the amount of bruising and wounding that day she would not have been able to walk properly. The defence suggested that Mary Ann had suffered a miscarriage, and that Harriet perhaps had attempted to help her evacuate the womb to both improve her health and save her reputation. Or that Mary Ann's friends and relations may have attempted to do the same, and subsequently accidentally caused her death.

The summing up of the case by the judge was as follows:

His Lordship, addressing the jury, said it was the law of England that a person who, pursuing a felonious intent, brought about the death of another person was guilty of murder. Thus, if this woman endeavoured to procure abortion and in doing so produced Mary Ann's death, it was murder. But if treating Mary Ann for an innocent purpose and not to procure abortion and death – through her unskilfulness – followed it was not murder but manslaughter. It was important to consider whether drugs and instruments had been used. The doctor had said that an instrument must have been used. Then who used it? Could the poor woman herself or her friends? No suspicion was associated with the friends; and it must be remembered that the deceased and the prisoner were in frequent association.

Whatever actually happened to Mary Ann, and the role of her mother and Harriet in the case, in the end, Harriet was found guilty of manslaughter by the jury. Her words on hearing the verdict were:

I am not guilty. I am entirely innocent. It is only a vile conspiracy on the part of (Mary Ann's mother) and her friends. Oh, my lord, I knew no more of her true condition than you did. Oh, my poor children, don't take me away from them.

It is hard, from a modern perspective, to read this case and not wonder if details were missed, and conclusions drawn on the part of each of the women involved that related to society and women's expected role within the social structure. Modern investigation and medical practices might also have had a bearing on the case. It may be that Harriet – reportedly a devout Baptist – was entirely innocent, and suffered a miscarriage of justice, or it may be that as a married woman with six children of her own she knew how not have another and applied that knowledge to Mary Ann. What is certain though is that Mary Ann's death was entirely accidental, and the villain of the piece is neither party, nor the man who made Mary Ann pregnant, but the society that they lived in that both denied women's sexuality and desire, and vilified women for acting upon them in an entirely natural manner.

Harriet was jailed for ten years for the manslaughter, and sent to Woking prison, many miles away in Surrey. Her husband remained local to Calne and Chippenham, bringing up their children. However, on 18 February 1890, seven years into her sentence, Harriet was declared insane and taken to Broadmoor Criminal Lunatic Asylum until a further order or the expiration of her sentence.

In 1893, when her original sentence ran out, Harriet was taken to the Wiltshire County Asylum at Devizes where she remained indefinitely.

It is from their records that we can decipher what had happened to her.

Her insistence of her innocence in the case that had convicted her had by this time become an obsession, and she had been therefore diagnosed of chronic mania with delusions of persecution.

The doctor reports:

> Says she is the victim of a conspiracy to deprive her of her liberty – that she is cruelly and shamefully treated by those in authority, preventing her husband and friends communicating with her or to make any effort to alleviate her sufferings: that her trial, sentence and consequent confinement are illegal.

Her confinement and treatment in prison, not surprisingly, appears to have had an extremely detrimental effect on her mental health. Harriet is the only patient at the time not to have a photograph included in the records – she apparently believed that if they took one they might use it against her to persecute her. Reports are that she believed the staff were against her, and that she was a force of good and others were wicked. She read and quoted from the Bible continually, and wrote to committees and asked to be released – which was denied. Victorian psychiatric care being what it was, there is no treatment recorded for Harriet and it appears that their plan was to lock her up until she gave up this insistence of her innocence. She never did.

She somehow collected money while in the asylum, which she intended to use to aid her escape, but it's unknown exactly where this money came from. There are three incidences of her being caught with money that she should not have had, once while bathing a sovereign disguised as a button was found in her clothes, and another time she was found to have bought epsom salts while out shopping with other inmates in Devizes.

Aside from her mental health, she apparently was a great sportswoman who had a real affinity with animals. She acted as the hospital rat catcher. She was also described as an ardent naturalist – which fits with her plant knowledge as a herbalist.

She was kept in the Wiltshire Asylum for 23 years past the end of her original sentence, and does not ever appear to have given up her claim of innocence. Release, when it occurred, appears to have been unremarkable. She had had some physical health issues and was quietly allowed to return to her husband in the summer of 1915, at the age of 75.

He had been living with his sister and her husband in Oxfordshire, working as a jobbing gardener. They had six years together before he died leaving his assets to her. After this she seems to have moved to Cefn Forest, in South Wales, to reside with a nephew – Mr Powell – where she was described as a 'young old lady' of 84 who was full of vim and vigour, and liked to take a cold bath every morning. She died there in 1924.

References

Adams, C (1982), *Ordinary Lives*, Virago Press

Bath Chronicle and Weekly Gazette, 28 June 1883, *Chippenham – The Serious Charge against a Herbalist*

Bath Chronicle and Weekly Gazette, 12 July 1883, *Wiltshire Assizes*

Devizes and Wilts Advertiser, 11 May 1882 *Inquest*

Devizes and Wilts Advertiser, 21 June 1883 *Serious Charge against An Herbalist*

Devizes and Wiltshire Gazette, 21 June 1883 *A sad and melancholy case*

Devizes and Wiltshire Gazette, 28 June 1883 *The manslaughter case at Chippenham*

Devizes and Wilts Advertiser, 12 July 1883 *The Charge of Murder by a Calne Herbalist*

Dundee Courier, 20 June 1883 *Charge of Murder*

England and Wales: Birth, Marriage and Death Records, held by Ancestry.co.uk

England and Wales: Christening Index 1530-1980, held by Ancestry.co.uk

England & Wales, Criminal Registers, 1791-1892, held by Ancestry.co.uk

England & Wales, Criminal Lunacy Warrant and Entry Books, 1882-1898, held by Ancestry.co.uk

Merthyr Express, 25 August 1923, *A Young Old Lady*

Portsmouth Evening News, 21 June 1883 *Alleged Murder by a Herbalist*

Records of Roundway Mental Hospital, Devizes, held by Wiltshire and Swindon History Centre

The Salisbury Times. 14 July 1883 *Wilts Summer Assizes*

The Salisbury Times, 14 July 1883, *The Chippenham Abortion Case*

Trowbridge Chronicle, 23 June 1883 *Serious Charge against an Herbalist*

Trowbridge Chronicle, 30 June 1883 *The Charge Against An Herbalist*

UK 1851 census, held by Ancestry.co.uk

UK 1861 census, held by Ancestry.co.uk

UK 1871 census, held by Ancestry.co.uk

UK 1881 census, held by Ancestry.co.uk

UK 1891 census, held by Ancestry.co.uk

UK 1901 census, held by Ancestry.co.uk

UK 1911 census, held by Ancestry.co.uk

UK 1921 census, held by Findmypast.co.uk

UK, Calendar of Prisoners, 1868-1929, held by Ancestry.co.uk

Warminster & Westbury journal, and Wilts County Advertiser, 30 June 1883 *The Serious Charge against a Herbalist*

Western Daily Press, 28 June 1883, *The Charge Against A Herbalist At Chippenham*

Wilts and Gloucestershire Standard, 23 June 1883, *Serious Charge against a Herbalist*

Wilts and Gloucestershire Standard, 14 July 1883, *Charge of Murder by a Calne Woman*

Wiltshire Asylum Registers, 1789-1921, held by Findmypast.co.uk

Wiltshire Baptisms Index 1530-1917, held by Findmypast.co.uk

Wiltshire, England, Church of England Births and Baptisms 1813-1916, held by Ancestry.co.uk

Wiltshire Times and Trowbridge Advertiser, 3 September 1904, *A Pauper Lunatic's Hoard*

Alice Elizabeth Lanham and Laura Julia Turner

T HERE WERE THREE Wiltshire signatories on the 1866 women's suffrage petition that was presented to Parliament that year, which marks the first official attempt to give women the vote in the UK. One of these was a Miss Cunnington from Devizes, the others were a pair of teachers – Miss Lanham and Miss Turner, from Corsham.

Miss Cunnington could have been one of about eight different women, though all sisters. There were many daughters of William and Elizabeth Cunnington, who were woolstaplers (dealers in wool) and lived at Southgate House in Devizes. By 1861, the last census before the petition was submitted, William had died but Eliza was living at home with four of her unmarried daughters – Eliza, Anne, Louisa and Letitia. Non-conformist baptisms for the area also reveal that there were four more daughters – Isabel, Emily, Maria and Jessie – as well as some sons. Since the signature came from a Miss Cunnington, it could not have been mother Elizabeth as she'd have been Mrs. The eldest daughter, Eliza, was just over 50 and unwed in 1866, and it may well have been her who signed in the interests of her younger siblings – but equally Miss Cunnington could have been Anne, Louisa, Letitia, Isabel or Maria, but less likely Emily or Jessie who had both married by that date.

In contrast, it is possible to pin point the exact identities of both Corsham teachers Miss Lanham and Miss Turner, and how they came to be in a position to sign the 1866 petition.

They were two of 1,499 women who signed. Due to the logistics, each woman signed separately and their signatures were pasted together into a long scroll, which was presented to parliament by John Stuart Mill – a well-known philosopher, and at this stage a Member of Parliament.

John Stuart Mill was the stepfather of Helen Taylor, who had been written to that May by campaigner Barbara Bodichon (who had published the *Brief Summary of the Laws of England concerning Women* in

1854, which was instrumental in paving the way towards the Married Women's Property Act of 1870) with the idea that they could work together to push for voting rights for women. John Stuart Mill had endorsed women's suffrage in his election campaign the previous year, so Barbara knew she'd at least get his attention. Helen told Barbara that the Reform Bill was currently under discussion, and that women who sought the vote should speak up, and if enough signatures were received her stepfather would present the petition to Parliament.

The two women embarked on a letter-writing campaign with five others – including Elizabeth Garrett, sister of Millicent Fawcett, and Emily Davies – and got the word out, deciding to ask for the rights of all householders rather than expressly for women. The petition asked Parliament:

> That it having been expressly laid down by high authorities that the possession of property in this country carries with it the right to vote in the election of Representatives in Parliament, it is an evident anomaly that some holders of property are allowed to use this right, while others, forming no less a constituent part of the nation, and equally qualified by law to hold property, are not able to exercise this privilege.
>
> That the participation of women in the Government is consistent with the British Constitution, inasmuch as women in these islands have always been capable of sovereignty, and women are eligible for various public offices.
>
> Your Petitioners therefore humbly pray your honourable House to consider the expediency of providing for the representation of all householders, without distinction of sex, who possess such property or rental qualification as your honourable House may determine
>
> And your Petitioners will ever pray.

It was to this that whichever Miss Cunnington of Devizes, and Alice and Laura of Corsham, signed their names and sent in to the fledgling committee. Barbara Bodichon was unable to present the petition due to illness, but Elizabeth Garrett and Emily Davies took it to John Stuart Mill, and the names were also circulated as a pamphlet.

He presented it to Parliament in July, and a year later there was the first parliamentary debate on votes for women. The motion was ultimately defeated, by 73 votes to 196, but the wheels, and the debate, had set the conversation in motion. Alice and Laura may not have known it at the time, but they were part of the momentum that led eventually to universal suffrage.

The road that led to their signatures began in Bath in the late 1820s. Alice, at this stage known as Elizabeth, was the older of the pair. She was baptised at Lyncombe and Widcombe, to the south of the centre of Bath, in March 1828, and was the daughter of baker John Lanham and his second wife Alice Salter. Laura was born a year or so later, also in Bath, to William Turner, a butcher, and his wife Mary Ann Gunning. On the surface, both of their father's professions seem fairly manual and not particularly monied, but these men were living and working in Bath as it was thriving and still had a booming tourist trade – and both seem to have been very comfortably off.

They grew up on either side of the River Avon through the city, initially without the barrier of the railway too. Alice lived at Widcombe Parade, probably above her father's baking business, which appears to have been extensive and founded by her grandfather. She had an array of siblings, some half-brothers from her father's first marriage and a few full brothers from her parents.

Laura was the youngest of a clutch of siblings who grew up in a profitable butchers' premises in Southgate Street. Unlike Alice, she had a surviving sister – Sarah Elizabeth – and several brothers. Her father died in 1835, when she was about 6, and her mother took over the butchering business alongside raising the children. They were comfortably off, and could afford servants and workers in the shop.

Alice, still officially called Elizabeth, lost her mother in 1844, when she was about 15. Her father followed in 1846, leaving a will that made financial provision for Alice and her two younger brothers as they were yet to reach the age of majority. He owned extensive property in St James Court, Bath, and at Coombe Down, which must have left a good financial cushion for his family. Alice's older brother Charles, at this point married and running a pub close by in Bath was to look after her and her brothers. However, she wasn't with them on the 1851 census, and there's no obvious trace of her. It may be that, given her later profession, she was working as a governess in someone's house, and her employers haven't recorded her details correctly.

In contrast, by 1851, Laura was visiting relatives of her brother's wife elsewhere in Bath, while her brother continued the butcher's business. She'd lost her mother the year before, and was taking in work as a dress maker. Her sister Sarah, on this census, said that she was a school mistress – so it may be that she gradually encouraged Laura to come into that fold too. However, Sarah did not continue as a teacher, and instead kept house for her brother before marrying in 1861. She and her new husband moved to Melksham, and raised several children.

Exactly when Alice and Laura encountered each other and came together to work isn't clear. They may have known each other since childhood, since they were of a similar social class and background, or they could have met in early womanhood. However, they had definitely formed a teaching partnership by the summer of 1860.

The first advert for Alice and Laura's school appeared in the *Hereford Journal* in July that year. Based at Belvedere House on Pickwick Road in Corsham, it is presented as a 'Ladies Boarding and Scholastic Establishment' which cost eight guineas per year to attend. To have afforded the school set up, Alice probably drew on her inheritance from her father. Both Alice and Laura are listed equally in the advert, with neither of them given the outright title of head of school, and this approach seems to have carried through all their work together.

Girls' boarding schools were still very much a new thing at this time. North London Collegiate School was established in 1850 and Cheltenham Ladies College been set up in 1853, and the idea was gradually being taken up – though the Belfast Ladies' Institute, often talked of as one of the earliest girls' boarding schools, was not founded until 1867. There are some USA boarding schools that have earlier foundation dates, and moves were being made in continental Europe too. In the UK, there were occasionally tiny girls' schools, that mostly took day pupils but might board one or two girls in the headteacher's house, earlier than this, but they were few and far between. Alice and Laura were part of a new movement to improve the formal education of young women by more rigorous means than a governess, and in a space that was more equal to that which young men experienced.

Families with money would generally send their sons to a boarding school to be educated after the age of about nine. Sometimes these were bigger institutions, like Eton or Repton or Marlborough, and sometimes they were smaller places set up in bigger houses – the sons of Chippenham engineer Rowland Brotherhood and his wife Priscilla attended a place like this in Calne, and there were several smaller settings with a handful of pupils in Chippenham too. Upper class girls, on the other hand, at this time were more often educated at home under a live-in governess, which was how many gently-bred unmarried women found their initial work, and was probably in Alice Lanham's background. This governess would educate the boys too, until they left for school at nine, but would teach the family's girls for as long as was felt necessary.

1860 was still nine years away from the Endowed Schools Act, which restructured some previously held educational conventions and distributions, and was instrumental in setting up more girls' schools – so Alice and Laura were acting independently in setting their school up. And it was twenty years away from the Education Act of 1880 which made it compulsory for all children to receive education between the ages of five and ten, whether they were boys or girls, and led to the establishment of more regular day schools. As Alice and Laura were acting independently of any official act or law, how and what they taught at Belvedere House was really up to them, and they were forging their own path.

Belvedere House is a name that does not appear to have endured with the property. At a best guess, given the path of the census enumerator in 1861, it appears to have been on the A4, somewhere near the Hare and Hounds pub junction that at that time was between Pickwick Road and Pickwick Street. Alice and Laura may have picked the name to give their school gravitas.

The 1861 census finds Alice and Laura in situ at their school in Corsham, both given as governesses, with an extra teacher living with them and four pupils ranging in age between 17 and 9. Particularly unusually for the time, Alice – as the older of the two – is listed as the head of the household, with Laura listed underneath her as her partner. Alice's entry is also particularly confusing, as she's given both her's and Laura's names as her own in one listing, ostensibly probably to emphasise the equality of their working partnership – although LGBTQ+ relationships between pairs of female teachers were not uncommon, even during this period, but would not have been portrayed as such. Alice uses Alice as her name on this document for the first visible time too, which may have been a childhood nickname that replaced Elizabeth – since she was the only surviving daughter of her parents' marriage – or could have been a later tribute to her mother. She used Alice or Alice Elizabeth in combination for the rest of her life. Her older brother Charles, who had been tasked in her father's will with looking after her, had taken up a position as the booking clerk at Corsham railway station around 1860, so founding a school in Corsham may have been at his suggestion.

The adverts for Alice and Laura's school continue, though mostly in more local papers. Belvedere House is given as a 'Ladies' Boarding

School' in various editions of the *Bath Chronicle and Weekly Gazette*, advertising term start dates and saying that their teaching was assisted by a French and English resident governess. This was presumably the Mary Susannah Roberts who was living with them on the 1861 census. They also say in the adverts that eminent masters attend the school. This would probably have been visiting male teachers who offered tuition in art, music and dance, as part of the wider curriculum they offer – as Alice and Laura would have handled the basic three Rs, history, geography, and ubiquitous religious instruction themselves.

A later inventory of their school lists all the accoutrements of a large middle-to-upper-class style house, presumably aimed at providing a home-from-home atmosphere for their young pupils. There are chimney ornaments, sofas, side boards and curtains listed alongside the beds and mattresses, desks, cloakroom furniture, globes, pianos, dumb bells and calisthenic equipment that would all have played their part in boarding school education at that time.

By mid-1862 they appear to have outgrown the Belvedere House premises, from which can be surmised that they then had considerably more pupils than the four visible on the census the year earlier. Adverts in the *Bath Chronicle and Weekly Gazette* say that they are moving their school to Claremont House, on Corsham's Melksham Road, described as a 'detached and commodious residence with ample pleasure grounds, and within a short distance of a railway station'.

Claremont House still exists, though it's been added to over the years. It sits on Prospect, which was Melksham Road at that time, and was triangular in shape and adjacent to the road. There were extensive

grounds that stretched towards The Lindleys, and it would have been spacious for the small school at that time. They operated the school from this house from July 1862 onwards.

Their subsequent adverts only seem to appear in the local press, so it appears that they could draw enough pupils from across Bath and its environs rather than looking further afield. By 1864 they were offering testimonials and prospectuses, and in 1865 their staff included a 'Parisienne' mistress – a French woman. French and Swiss governesses were prized teachers of young women, partly as they were fluent in French and therefore could pass that skill on to their pupils, and partly because the French and Swiss systems did offer some formal instruction in how to educate. Alice and Laura were always referred to equally in the school adverts, both called Lady Principals, with neither given more weight that the other.

It was against this formal education background, running their own business and furthering the learning of young women, that Alice and Laura decided to sign Barbara Bodichon and Helen Taylor's suffrage petition in May 1866. They would have been resident at Claremont when their signatures were sent in to be used on the scroll.

However, that December, their partnership was suddenly dissolved and the school would be run by their successors. A message in the *Bath Chronicle and Weekly Gazette* on 10 January 1867 announced that their work together had ceased on 21 December.

The reason for this is immediately obvious from the death records, as Alice Lanham died on 13 January 1867. She must have known that this was coming, and dissolving the partnership with Laura would have been a way of settling her affairs. Laura was present at, and certified Alice's death – which her certificate gives as cancer. Whether she was a platonic partner or a romantic partner, the women would have been very close, and she will have lost a trusted friend.

For Alice, and indeed any physician who treated her, to have known she was suffering from cancer at this time, her tumour(s) must have been obvious. Physicians' texts mention cancer, and its treatments, from quite early on – for example, Lady Johanna St John of Lydiard, near Swindon, had a recipe book from the 17th century that had concoctions to treat breast cancer. However, to have known it was a cancer that afflicted Alice, the diagnosis would have involved various physical changes and obvious lumps, which the physician would have recognised and would probably not have been spotted if it was internal.

Cancer treatment at this time would mostly have been about appeasing the symptoms rather than attempting cure the disease outright. There was some idea, which stemmed from use of a microscope, that the illness spread from the initial tumour site via the blood or lymph system, but this was not formally written down until the early 1870s by English surgeon Campbell De Morgan, which was too late for Alice in 1866/7. Removal of tumours came along later, but carried complications due to instrument hygiene which was still not fully understood.

Alice was buried in Bath, close to her parents, and given as the daughter of the late John Lanham. Her brother Charles continued to live in Corsham, and became the railway station master.

Laura sold the school at Claremont House, and all of their educational equipment, to the Misses Butler in the February following Alice's death. The Butlers had their version of the school ready to go by at least the May of 1869, and began advertising.

Laura, meanwhile, left Corsham and became a governess. Without Alice's partnership to support her, she took the usual route of an educated and older unmarried woman who needed to make a living. The 1871 census finds her as a governess in Tenterden, Kent, instructing the children of a brewer and wine merchant. Two years later, Laura married William James – a widowed wine merchant who she may have met through her previous employer – in Bath.

Exactly what happened to Laura next is unclear. She's not immediately visible on the 1881 census, and again may have been working somewhere where her details were not accurately recorded. Her husband's name is also so common that without a birth date estimate – he's recorded as just 'of full age' i.e. over 21 on their marriage certificate – he's not really traceable on that document either. On the 1891 census, however, she appears as a widowed music teacher boarding in Streatham, so is back earning her own living through teaching. By 1901 she seems to have given up the teaching, but is still boarding in London – this time in Lambeth with a carpenter and his family. She died in the Autumn of 1907, while the beginnings of the WSPU campaign to gain the vote that she'd supported in her youth were rumbling, and was buried in Lambeth.

The school she'd helped to found with Alice continued, however. Under the Butlers – widowed Sarah Butler, who came from Bath via Horton in Gloucester kept the school, but her daughters Sara and Rose were listed as the main governesses on the 1871 census - Claremont

House Ladies College continued to offer 'a thorough education, combined with home comforts', according to an advert in 1876. There were ten students aged between nine and 13 listed on the 1871 census. References to the rigours of education expected start to creep into their marketing, as by 1880 they state that their pupils will be prepared for the Local Examinations – qualifications set by the University of Cambridge from 1858 onwards, held at local centres that proved that pupils had been educated to a particular standard but not to university level.

Sara Butler married a Swiss professor of modern languages, who had probably come to teach at Claremont in 1877. The same year, Rose Butler also married and went to live in London. Mother Sarah was left as the principal of the school by the 1881 census, with only one (male) pupil, and there's an advert for Mrs Emma A Butler putting the school and its contents and equipment up for sale in March 1881.

It was bought by a Miss Shaw, who had established herself as head mistress, with a Miss Sherburne as her second – which brought to an end an equal partnership of women at the head of the school. By 1884 they were advertising preparation for Higher Examinations alongside the Locals, which would prepare their pupils if they wanted to continue their education at universities – which were just starting to open up to women, even if neither Oxford or Cambridge would admit women to degrees. Miss Sherburne left and was replaced by Miss Chrystal, and by 1885 a Mrs Milne was at the helm.

In April 1885 widowed Mrs Caroline Milne advertised her school in Northern Ireland, saying that the education that she provided was high class, and that the students were regularly prepared for the Cambridge Local and College Preceptors, and that all who had entered these at Christmas had passed successfully. The *Bristol Mercury* reported a successful prize giving at the school in 1889, still under Mrs Milne, where the pupils performed music and drama as part of the entertainment. The school had 22 pupils on the 1891 census, all aged between 13 and 18. Agnes Tennant joined Caroline as a joint principal by 1895, and the school was again under dual female leadership as it had originally been founded by Alice and Laura.

The school was still a going concern in 1920, but Claremont House was a private home by 1923. By 1973, the building had been added to and adapted, and was being used as retirement home. It continues in that purpose today.

References

American Cancer Society (2024) The Cancer Atlas: History of Cancer, at https://canceratlas.cancer.org/history-cancer/19th-century/ (accessed 17.1.2024)

Bath Chronicle and Weekly Gazette, 18 July 1861 *Belvedere House*

Bath Chronicle and Weekly Gazette, 26 December 1861 *Belvedere House*

Bath Chronicle and Weekly Gazette, 2 January 1862 *Belvedere House*

Bath Chronicle and Weekly Gazette, 13 March 1862 *Belvedere House*

Bath Chronicle and Weekly Gazette, 10 July 1862 *Notice of removal*

Bath Chronicle and Weekly Gazette, 4 September 1862 *Tuition: Notice of removal*

Bath Chronicle and Weekly Gazette, 23 June 1864 *Ladies' Boarding School*

Bath Chronicle and Weekly Gazette, 19 January 1865 *Claremont House, Corsham, Wilts*

Bath Chronicle and Weekly Gazette, 13 July 1865 *Ladies' Boarding School*

Bath Chronicle and Weekly Gazette, 10 January 1867 *Tuition*

Bath Chronicle and Weekly Gazette, 7 February 1867 *Claremont House near Corsham, Wilts*

Bristol Mercury, 19 December 1889, *Corsham*

Busher, H (1986) *Education since 1800,* History in Depth series, Macmillan Education

Crawford, E (2013) *The Women's Suffrage Movement in Britain and Ireland: A Regional Survey*, Routledge

Devizes and Wilts Advertiser, 7 February 1867 *Claremont House near Corsham, Wilts*

Devizes and Wiltshire Gazette, 30 April 1885, *Ladies' school*

England & Wales, Non-Conformist and Non-Parochial Registers, 1567-1936, held by Ancestry.co.uk

England & Wales, Prerogative Court of Canterbury Wills, 1384-1858, held by Ancestry.co.uk

Enniskillen Chronicle and Erne Packet, 6 April 1885 *Ladies' school*

Hereford Journal, 18 July 1860, *Belvedere House*

Marlborough Times, 12 March 1881 *Claremont House Corsham*

Marlborough Times, 19 January 1884 *Ladies' College, Claremont House, Corsham, near Bath*

Murphy, G. (2016) *The 1866 Women's Suffrage Petition*, at https://blogs.lse.ac.uk/lsehistory/2016/06/07/the-1866-womens-suffrage-petition/

North Wilts Herald, 15 May 1876 *Claremont House Corsham*

North Wilts Herald, 12 August 1876 *Claremont House Corsham*

North Wilts Herald, 30 August 1880 *Claremont House Corsham*

Selin, S. (2017) Cancer Treatment in the 19th Century, at https://shannonselin.com/2017/08/cancer-treatment-19th-century/ (accessed 17.1.2024)

Somerset, England, Church of England Baptisms, 1813-1914, held by Ancestry.co.uk

Somerset, England, Church of England Baptisms, Marriages, and Burials, 1531-1812, held by Ancestry.co.uk

Somerset, England, Marriage Registers, Bonds and Allegations, 1754-1914, held by Ancestry.co.uk

UK and Ireland, Find a Grave® Index, 1300s-Current, held by Ancestry.co.uk

UK, City and County Directories, 1766 - 1946, held by Ancestry.co.uk

UK Parliament (2024) *Presenting the 1866 petition* at https://www.parliament.uk/about/living-heritage/transformingsociety/electionsvoting/womenvote/parliamentary-collections/1866-suffrage-petition/presenting-the-petition/

Whalley, P (2009) *Claremont Ladies College & Claremont Nursing Home, The Linleys, Corsham*, at https://www.corshamcivicsociety.co.uk/wp-content/uploads/2015/07/2009-NOVEMBER.pdf (accessed 17.1.2024)

Wiltshire County Mirror, 5 May 1869 *Claremont House, Corsham, Wilts*

Wilts and Gloucestershire Standard, 5 April 1884 *Ladies' College, Claremont House, Corsham, near Bath*

Lilian Young or Yeates

T HE RAILWAY AGE is often seen as a romantic one, with clouds of steam and breathless brief encounters perhaps eclipsing the reality of filthy hard work and clothes full of soot smuts. However, the community around railways could at least partly be described as romantic in that many people met their partners among the multifarious professions employed on and around the rails.

Lilian Young, later Yeates, was one of these, as she came from a railway family, and married a railway man. However, where her tale differs is that she did not remain associated with the rails and instead became landlady of a pub.

She was born in Bristol, the second child of railway platelayer – someone who inspected the conditions of the track – George Young and his wife Minnie in 1893. Six younger siblings followed, and the family grew up beside the harbour railway in Bristol's docklands area, alongside boats working with tobacco, coal, chocolate and other heavy industry.

In her teens her father moved to a similar role on the Strawberry Line or the Cheddar Valley Line, and the family went with him. Cheddar would have had far more country freedom and better fresh air than the industrial heart of Bristol, and ought to have been a pleasant move. The railway line was known as the Strawberry Line because it primarily transported the famous Cheddar strawberries from the area to be bought in shops all over the UK, and would have made a big change from the cargos in Bristol.

Upon leaving school Lilian found work as a waitress in a restaurant, quite possibly in Cheddar station café, and boarded out of the family home. As a waitress she would probably have been expected to do a lot of clearing and cleaning of the premises, as well as serving food. Station buffets were known for serving dishwatery tea and cakes to sustain travellers as they made their connections, as the railway network was far wider and more complicated than today.

In 1912 Lilian came to Chippenham, a town with a strong railway industry, to run the station buffet. This would have meant a step up from waitressing, as she was in charge of ordering and preparing all the food and drink at a main line railway station directly linked to London, and she would probably have had some staff working under her management. She lived on Station Hill in a set of a few cottages that looked directly down the hill. These were demolished in the 1960s.

By 1915 she had met and married her husband Charles Yeates, a popular railway guard who was more than ten years her senior. He was known to be a staunch trade unionist, and a longtime member of the Chippenham lodge of the Royal Antediluvian Order of Buffaloes. Initially they lived behind the town's Westinghouse brake and signalling works at Hawthorn Road, and their first son Ewart followed later that year, with another – Aubrey – born five years later. The gap in their children's ages would perhaps suggest that her husband served in the first world war in some capacity, but there is no obvious evidence for this.

Meanwhile, her older sister Alice had also married a railway man, and had moved to Devizes for a time. Her husband George ran the signals for that branch of the Great Western Railway. They later moved to Swindon, then Worthing on the south coast during the war. A younger brother, Sidney, became a dairy farmer just south of Bath.

Things changed for Lilian in early 1932 when they bought a pub, the Old Road Inn (later Tavern) – including all the fixtures, fittings and cutlery, and even including the 60 tulip bulbs in the garden – which was one of two frequented by railway workers and those employed in the next-door bacon factory. This was just behind Chippenham's railway station, and had several rooms – a bar, smoking room, club room, drawing room, and kitchen with meat safes. Lilian had previously been employed by the former landlord, Mr Cockram (whose family had had the pub since the 1890s), to run the catering side of his business, so it seemed an obvious choice for her to become the next manager.

Her husband, who had long been employed on the railway, kept his job as a railway guard while being landlord at the pub. However, in practice with him employed down the road – despite gaps in trains arriving and departing the station, and the pub being only a stone's throw away – it would have been Lilian who would have opened the bar for trade and served the beer, in addition to providing any food that the pub would serve and keeping the place clean and tidy. She was aided in her landlady's role by her two sons, but they also had jobs elsewhere – one at the post office and telephone exchange and the other at the town's nearby bacon factory. Despite this huge amount of work, and her official role as landlady, the 1939 register tersely gives Lilian's profession as 'unpaid domestic duties at home'.

As publicans, the family were well integrated into town life. The pub was regarded as home territory for many local organisations and clubs, and her eldest son – a pianist – even had his own band that provided local entertainment at functions and dances.

A year into World War II, her husband died – only in his late 50s – and Lilian ran the pub alone with the help of her sons. However, with pressure to join up and fight her eldest son Ewart went into the air force not long after his father's death. He was killed in a flying accident, when he flew into a tree, around nine months later. Some reports say this was at Sherston, others that it was at Norton. He was awaiting his wings, and was 26 years old, and was engaged to a woman named Dorothy Short. This left Lilian with two close bereavements within a year of each other.

Her younger son Aubrey did go away on war duties, but not to the air force. Needing extra help to run the pub, a bar manager-of-sorts moved in to help Lilian. This was Temple John Jenkins, known as John or 'Uncle John' to her grandchildren, and was clearly Lilian's special friend – but she never married him.

Aubrey, who had continued to work as a Post Office and Telephone Engineer after the war, married in 1950, and went to live elsewhere with his bride Pat.

Lilian's dairy farmer brother Sidney used to regularly bring his stock to Chippenham market via the train station close to Lilian's pub. Another brother, Bernard, was killed in a quarry truck accident in the mid-1950s, in the Cheddar area. Lilian is mentioned as a mourner at both of their funerals.

Local railway men treated the pub as their own space for business and social functions. It was also headquarters for many other organisations, societies and social groups, much in the way that the local Chippenham Town Morris dancers treat the space as their own today.

Lilian continued to run the pub, now landlady in name as well as action, alongside John until 1957, when she retired and moved with John to Yewstock Crescent. It is unclear whether part of the land that the pub owned, which fronted Chippenham's New Road, was sold by Lilian or the next incumbents of the pub.

In retirement, Lilian continued to live a busy life and was still involved in the affairs of the town. Her grandchildren remember visiting her and 'Uncle John' at Yewstock Crescent, being taken out in a swish car, and her doting on her beloved dogs.

She died around a decade after she retired, and is buried alongside her husband and elder son in the grounds of the church in which she married – St Paul's on Malmesbury Road – within spitting distance of her former pub.

References

Bristol, England, Church of England Baptisms, 1813-1922, held by Ancestry. co.uk

Electoral registers for Chippenham, 1912-1958, held by Wiltshire and Swindon History Centre

England and Wales: Birth, Marriage and Death Records, held by Ancestry.co.uk

England and Wales: Christening Index 1530-1980, held by Ancestry.co.uk

Jefferies, S (1987), *A Chippenham Collection*, Chippenham Civic Society

Quartley, Son and White Valuation books, 1932, held by Wiltshire and Swindon History Centre

UK census collection, held by Ancestry.co.uk

Western Daily Press, Friday 30 August 1940. *Chippenham funeral of Mr C. J. Yeates*

Wiltshire Times and Trowbridge Advertiser, 2 August 1941. *Airman's death. L/A/C Ewart Yeates*

Wiltshire Times and Trowbridge Advertiser, 22 July 1950. *Weddings. Mr Aubrey Yeates and Miss Pat Watts*

Wiltshire Times and Trowbridge Advertiser, 19 November 1955. *Friend of many. Retirement of popular licensee*

Wiltshire Times and Trowbridge Advertiser, 26 November 1955. *Old Road Inn*

Ann Colborne or Salway

A LTHOUGH WOMEN BECOMING doctors did not happen until well into the 19th century (Bristol-born Elizabeth Blackwell graduated from medical school in the USA in 1849, London's Elizabeth Garrett Anderson became a doctor on home soil in 1865, and Dr James Barry, born c1789, spent the first 20 years of his life presenting as female), there were still a few women who worked in healthcare in less prestigious roles.

The tradition of a wise woman, or herbalist, stretches back through time. She would have dispensed folk remedies and health care advice for a lesser price than a doctor (no NHS back then), and would have often been the first port of call for women's health problems.

It was rarer, although no way unheard of, to find a woman who worked as a chemist or druggist, which had more of a medical science nuance to the work and profession. This was a role more often performed by men. However, Chippenham's Ann Colborne, née Salway, operated as a druggist on the town's high street for many years in her own right, in the early 19th century. In common with other women who had this position, she had inherited the business from her husband when he died.

Ann had been the wife of town druggist and apothecary William Colborne, who was from a notable local medical family that had grown out of the village of Lacock. They were part of the family that owned Hardenhuish House at that time, but from a different branch. His father Robert Colborne, first cousin of Joseph Colborne of Hardenhuish, had been an apothecary. In 1753 Robert Colborne had published a medical text: *The Plain English Dispensatory: Containing the Natural History and Medicinal Virtues of the Principal Simples Now in Use. Also All the Compositions in the Three Dispensatories of London, Edinburgh, and Dr. Fuller.* This was presumably the main text that William Colborne used when he set himself up as an apothecary like his father. On William's death he had left his shop, drugs and medicines to Ann for her to continue practicing medicine and dispensing if she so wished. She did.

Ann had been born in 1760 in Corsham, to John and Sarah Salway. Baptism records of this time do not give father's profession, but it's likely that the family were fairly well off and in good social standing given who she married. She had a brother, Edward, who proved his mother's will in 1780, so she'd lost her mother by the age of 20.

Her marriage to William took place in 1779, in Chippenham's parish church. They had three children in fairly quick succession – Sarah in 1781, Frances in 1783 and William in 1785. Most women at this time would have had more than just three children, so the fact that Ann didn't perhaps indicates why she had more time than others to help her husband out with his work and learn his methods and medicine. This would have been the only formal training she had. The practice at the beginning of her career was unregulated, and the eventual Pharmacy Act of 1868 had 223 women added to the first register for the whole country.

The *Universal British Directory* of 1791 gives William Colborne as an apothecary and druggist, one of five under that job title in the town. Others under the title 'physic' are described as surgeon, apothecary and man-midwife. Ann is not mentioned as having the role at this stage. Just two years after this, William died. Ann was left with three children aged 12, 10 and 8, as well as William's business.

She did not have to take on the business if she didn't want to. William had bought their Market Place-based house outright, allocated her any rent she might draw from it, and had enough money to pay her and the children an amount of money each year that if it was wisely invested should have easily seen her through.

His will, made in 1791 and proved in 1794, says:

And also my stock of drugs and medicines and shop fixtures if my said wife Ann Colborne shall continue to carry on the business of a druggist but in case she refuses carrying on the said business then I direct my executors hereinafter named to sell and dispose thereof for the most money that they can obtain for the same and the money arising by the sale there if I desire maybe applied towards the putting of my said son William Colborne an apprentice to whatsoever business he may chose as soon as he shall arrive at a proper age.

It speaks volumes that, even though Ann had no need to take over William's business, she chose to continue to be the town's apothecary and druggist. It indicates that she must have enjoyed the work and found

it her calling. She ran the business for another thirty or so years.
She's given as Widow Colborne on the Land Tax records of 1798. The
business was also successful enough to pay for her son William to train as
a doctor. He is referred to as a surgeon by 1808, and practiced alongside
his mother in Chippenham.

Much of Ann's (and William's) working life would have been
making and dispensing remedies for all sorts of maladies. It could have
been anything from easing diarrhoea to making a salve to attempt to
treat breast cancer, and anything in between. Probably involving a lot of
bloodletting.

While the main medical text in use at the time was *A Book of
Phisick*, which dated initially from 1710 and was added to over the next
century or so, it is likely that Ann would have used her father-in-law's
book *The Plain English Dispensatory...* in her work as a druggist, as this
book was more relevant to that role than that of a physician or doctor.
It's held by the Wellcome Collection today. Ann's remedies would have at
least have been based on the advice and ideas given in this book, if not
following them closely.

The Plain English Dispensatory... has advice on preparing particular
different ingredients that could be used to treat patients. For example, it
examines the older procedure for preparing fox lungs for medicine, which
was:

> Take the Lungs of a Fox newly killed, and after they are separated from
> the Blood-vessels, wash them in White-wine wherein Hyssop and
> Scabious have been first boiled, then gently dry them in a Pan or Pot
> without burning; lastly, keep them for Use wrapped up in dry Hyssop,
> Wormwood, or Horehound.

Further on, the book has advice on how to make oil of earthworms:

> Oleum Lumbricorum. Oil of Earthworms. Take of Earthworms, well
> washed, half a Pound; of ripe Oil-olive, a Quart, and of White-wine, half
> a Pint: Boil them together in a Bath-heat till the Wine is consumed, then
> strain it out by Pressure. E.
>
> This has long been a Dispensatory Composition, and is kept in some
> Shops: It may be used for the same Purposes for which the above Oil of St
> John's Wort is recommended.

The book recommends St John's Wort oil for *'Bruises, cold, watry Swellings, gouty and rheumatic Pains; a little of it being rubbed into the Part.'*

Ann's tools were therefore a vast array of various herbs and plants, spiced wines and oils, many types of animal dung, urine taken from people and animals. Many of these ingredients she would have prepared herself. Rarer and hard to obtain ingredients might have been ordered from the garden run by the Company of Worshipful Apothecaries in London, which still exists today as the Chelsea Physic Garden. There would also have been appendages – penises, legs, bones on display in the shop, and various exotic powdered substances. The recipe lists for these cures from *The Book of Phisick* sound more like ingredients of classic witches' potions than medicines, but these methods would have been passed down from practitioner to practitioner, and there would have been no scientific testing or controlled trials in the way medicine does today.

On top of all this, Ann would also have provided basic first aid. She'd have dressed wounds and provided salves. The heavier work – amputations etc – would have been performed by her son William after he trained and qualified as a doctor, as that was considered doctoring. Some of the cures were aimed at livestock too. There's a reference in an edition of the *Bath Chronicle and Weekly Gazette* from 20 May 1802 to her stocking Bellamy's Medicine for the cure of Scouring Cattle.

Her daughter Frances had married a man called John in 1804, and went off to live with him in various different local places – a son was born the following year in Bath, a daughter in a Salisbury Plain village in 1812, and she eventually settled in Devizes.

An Apothecaries Act in 1815 gave practitioners like Ann the licence to practice and regulate medicine, and started to build on the more serious standing of their job in the medical profession. Ann, because she had worked so long at this stage but had no formal training, would not have been part of the Company of Worshipful Apothecaries. However, she'd have personally benefited from the increased legitimacy that this act gave the profession.

Ann's son William, who she lived with, married Sarah Taylor in 1818. She was the daughter of a Chippenham clothier, who were important within the cloth-producing business that ran the local economy. William in this year was 33 and a surgeon. He was apparently much loved as a doctor by much of the Chippenham population.

Ann is given as a druggist, alongside William, on the first proper trade directory of Wiltshire – *Pigot's Directory of Wiltshire* – in 1822. She would have been 62 and still working. This would have been considered elderly for the time. A trade directory was a sort of telephone book for an area, but obviously without the telephone numbers at this time as it was long off the time they were invented. They informed people coming into the area who was available for particular life services – lawyers, builders, wheelwrights and so on – and was a way of advertising for more business.

Her son William, as the town doctor, was involved in treating victims of the Chippenham Riot in 1822. That September, men from Kington Langley and Langley Burrell came to the town to confront some men from Chippenham who they felt had snubbed them at a recent market day. This turned into violence, and injuries, and two men were killed in the action. William Colborne deposed that he'd been pulled from bed to examine someone bleeding to death on the road from Chippenham to Bath. This turned out to be Joseph Hull, the town saddler, who was sadly dead at the roadside. It is likely Ann's drugs were used to treat the injuries of other riot victims.

Ann was also in the same druggist and apothecary position in the 1830 *Pigot's Directory*, when she had reached the age of 70. Son William, as well as working as a surgeon, was also attributed in the druggist business.

Her daughter Sarah, who had never married, died in her late 40s in 1831. She had apparently had a severe illness for a long time. Her daughter Francis also died in 1838, over in Devizes.

By the time of the 1839 *Robson's trade directory*, Ann had taken retirement and was not operating as a druggist anymore.

The 1841 census finds Ann aged 80, living with her son William and his family – he had nine children in the end – on the town high street. They were probably collecting rent on the house in the Market Place. William was working as a surgeon, and his son William Henry was training to be a doctor, so the family medical profession was continuing.

Ann died in the early part of 1843, aged 82. She was living on the High Street, with her son and his family. She was buried in St Andrew's churchyard, and her son William paid the death duty. He went on practicing medicine in St Mary Street, and became mayor of Chippenham in 1851. His son William, the third to have that name, also became a doctor and surgeon but died of locally-contracted typhoid in 1869, leaving a wife and seven children.

After this, the family left Chippenham and went to live in Kent, with some modern family members now in Australia. Ann's legacy was that her female descendants were always well educated, and several of them were early women recipients of university degrees.

References

Adams, C (1982) *Ordinary Lives*, Virago Press

Bath Chronicle and Weekly Gazette, 3 June 1802 *Bellamy's Restorative Medicine for the Cure of Scouring Cattle*

Bath Chronicle and Weekly Gazette, 3 March 1831 *Died*

Bath Chronicle and Weekly Gazette, 3 May 1832 *Sandwell's Issue Plasters*

Bath Chronicle and Weekly Gazette, 27 January 1870, *Dr W H Colborne, Deceased*

Bristol Mercury, Monday 16 September 1822, *Murderous affray at Chippenham*

Church & State Gazette (London), Friday 18 August 1843 *London*

Colborne, R (1753) *The Plain English Dispensatory,* Welcome Collection

Dorset County Chronicle, Thursday 23 July 1846 *Salisbury: - Wednesday July 22*

England and Wales: Birth, Marriage and Death Records, held by Ancestry.co.uk

England and Wales: Christening Index 1530-1980, held by Ancestry.co.uk

Daniell, J.J (1894), *The History of Chippenham*, R F Houlston

Jefferies, S (1987), *A Chippenham Collection*, Chippenham Civic Society

Pigot's Directory of Wiltshire (1822, 1830, 1842)

Probate records of the Archdeaconry of Wiltshire, held by Ancestry.co.uk

Robson's Directory (1839)

Salisbury and Winchester Journal, Monday 27 February 1809 *Salisbury*

Star (London), Monday 22 June 1807, *A caution to families &c, Cock's Reading Sauce for Fish*

The Universal British Directory (1791)

UK census collection, held by Ancestry.co.uk

Wiltshire, England, Church of England Births and Baptisms 1813-1916, held by Ancestry.co.uk

Wiltshire, England, Church of England Deaths and Burials, 1813-1916, held by

Ancestry.co.uk

Wiltshire, England, Church of England Marriages and Banns, 1754-1916, held
by Ancestry.co.uk

Wiltshire, England, Wills and Probate, 1530-1858, held by Ancestry.co.uk

Lady Muriel Coventry or Howard

M URIEL, ALSO KNOWN as Lady Coventry, has a street named after her – rare for a woman – in the area of Chippenham she was once Lady of the Manor for. Her achievements, as a prominent female member of the town Poor Law Board of Guardians, and only the second female magistrate the town had ever had in 1928, appear to have come in second to the extreme benevolence and generosity that she showed towards the impoverished residents of Chippenham. Lady Coventry Road, however, relates to the name she took when she married in 1893, and she was born a Howard and was a Lady from the get-go.

Born Mary Muriel Sophie Howard, she came from the family that produced Katherine Howard, fifth wife of King Henry VIII, but her branch split off in Tudor times. She was the eldest child of the 18th Earl of Suffolk and 11th Earl of Berkshire Henry Charles Howard, and as the daughter of an earl and a lord was entitled to call herself Lady her entire life, regardless of who she married. In the run up to her parents' marriage her father had been Member of Parliament for Malmesbury, located at the family seat at vast Charlton Park, to the north of the town. However, two years before Muriel arrived he had been defeated in the general election, so was taking a bit of break from political life.

Muriel was born in central London in 1870, and was baptised in Pimlico. She was followed less than two years later by a sister who didn't live long enough to be named. Her next sister, Eleanor, followed just over a year later, when the family were living in Rutland, and then another – Agnes – midway through 1874 when they were back in Wiltshire. The son and heir to continue the earldom, Henry, was born in Scotland, and then Muriel's final two siblings – Katherine and James – in Malmesbury in the 1880s.

Both brothers were sent away to school to be educated, as would have been common for sons of the nobility at this time – both attended Winchester College. Muriel and her sisters, however, appear to have been educated at home at Charlton Park. One census has a Scottish governess in the household, who is clearly in charge of educating the young ladies. It is always possible that Muriel attended some sort of formal finishing school before she made her societal debut, but there is no definite record of this.

She'd have made a formal debut at around 18, being presented at court to the queen as would have been expected for the daughter of an Earl, and would have officially entered the marriage market. This didn't happen immediately for her, however, and the 1891 census finds her still at home near Malmesbury at the age of 21, so she probably enjoyed several London social seasons. The household at Charlton Park included a cook, a couple of lady's maids, a footman, a butler, housemaids and kitchen maids, and even a still room maid – in charge of herbs and brewing for them all.

At the age of 23, Muriel married her first cousin – Henry Robert Beauclerk Coventry, the son of her mother's brother. Though marriage of first cousins is frowned upon today in the UK, mostly for genetic reasons, this was a common practice among the gentry in Victorian times. He was two years her junior, and had been a serving soldier. It's likely she already knew him, rather than meeting him through society, but it still would have been an advantageous match. He came from a prominent Scottish family, and a divorce scandal involving his mother in the late 1870s was temporally far away enough to be forgotten. They married at the church closest to Charlton Park, and initially lived close by, but in 1894 took on the vacant Monkton House in Chippenham. This Georgian-remodelled property had traditionally been the seat of the Esmead and Edridge families, and indeed was still owned by one of their descendants, but until 1892 had been the rented home of prominent local solicitor West Awdry and his family. His death left the house available for Muriel and Henry.

The first mention of her at Monkton House is as the honourable secretary of the Chippenham branch of the Soldiers and Sailor Family Association in 1894. All of the office holders were women from big houses and prominent families in the area, and the organisation helped both serving men in the forces and their dependent families. She also first joined the Chippenham Poor Law Board of Guardians in that year, alongside her husband, which was another function that was often filled by the wealthy and good of the town. However, in Muriel's case it proved to be less of a duty and more of a passion.

Boards of Guardians were a group of local officials – usually the great and the good of the area – who were responsible for overseeing the union workhouse and the provision for the poor of a civil parish. Under the Local Governance Act of 1894 the property qualification for election to the group was abolished, and it was possible for women to join the board, so Muriel would have been one of the first women to sit with them. They were responsible for overseeing all poor relief and assessing applications for it, maintaining the workhouse and appointing staff to its key positions, and working with the church wardens who collected the rate money to fund the work. They seem to have met either weekly or fortnightly at Chippenham.

Muriel did not have children for a few years after her marriage, but at the end of 1897 her daughter Joan was born, and she was followed by sons Dan and Arthur at two and four years afterwards. They were all baptised at the Charlton Park church, and appear to have been close to their mother's family.

All three children appear to have been sent away to be educated once they were old enough. Invariably, at this time, most children of the gentry were taught at home by a governess until they reached the age of nine, and then went away to school.

Muriel and Henry were far from alone while they were gone, however. Their household in 1911 had a clutch of servants – a cook, a lady's maid, a nurse, a house maid, a kitchen maid and two parlour maids. This was considerably fewer household staff than Muriel had grown up with, which may reflect a downturn in their fortunes, but equally could be explained by Monkton House being considerably smaller than Charlton Park, and therefore needing less people to keep the household going.

One of Muriel and her husband's first loves in the life of the town was music, and they actively supported orchestral work in the local area. Muriel had her own orchestral group, and brought them to many light operatic productions in the town. Both she and her husband were prominent members of the Poor Law Board of Guardians, with Muriel taking the position of Vice-Chairman of the Board for a time and though she was offered the position of Chairman she declined it. When the workhouse, the focus of the Board of Guardians, became the Chippenham Public Assistance Institution in 1930 following a change of legislation, she was nominated to represent the institution on the county council. Later, she beat Ralph Pearce in a by-election for the vacant Langley seat on the county council in 1932, and represented the area formally too, holding on to the seat in 1937. Her achievements as county councillor are largely unreported, as she mostly still appears in records in her other public works capacities. The council at that time directed interest and funds towards public institutions across the county, so she would have represented the Langley area in matters concerning schools, roads, hospitals and other infrastructure.

During the First World War she was involved in the Food Control Committee, ensuring that everyone locally had enough to eat, and in 1914 was on the board providing accommodation for Belgian refugees fleeing the conflict. Her daughter Joan, like many other upper-class women of the age, volunteered at the local field hospital and became a staff nurse treating wounded soldiers. Neither of her sons were old enough to fight in that conflict, but Arthur went into the navy straight after the war. Her brother Henry, however, who had become the next earl of the death of their father in 1898 and married a blue-blood American woman, was not so lucky and was killed by flying shrapnel in 1917 while serving in modern-day Iraq.

Two of her three sisters and other brother had married equally well (the third sister remained unmarried her whole life). Her mother, after she was widowed, left the big house and moved to a cottage on the Charlton Park estate.

In 1919, a descendant of the Esmead and Edridge families, Miss Carrick Moore, sold the Monkton House buildings and all the estates. Muriel and Henry, who had only rented the house until this point, bought the property that they lived in and all the surrounding land. Lady Muriel is referred to as the owner, rather than Henry, so it is probable that it was her inherited money that bought the estate.

Muriel was deeply involved in the provision that the Chippenham workhouse, later called the Institution, made for those in poverty. The general feeling among the place was that she treated the premises as her own house, and would often work tirelessly to improve the lives of those who resided there. She knew that many of the young women who grew up there and were placed in domestic service had nowhere to call home and return to during their time off, so she provided and furnished a large sitting room at the institution for their use, so they had somewhere comfortable to return to. She also provided a new organ for the workhouse chapel in 1917, and kept it maintained.

In 1928 she became only the second female magistrate to ever sit on the Chippenham bench, and regularly worked in local law matters, preferring public assistance cases and working in out-relief, but presiding over anything from pub licence renewals to minor motoring offences. She also had a considerable interest in the town hospital, and nursing association, sat on the parochial council of one of the churches, and was a manager of the local schools before they were taken over by the county council.

She was known to be a fan of collecting clocks. A 1933 issue of the *Liverpool Echo* reported that she owned over 100, all in working order, which required an hour's winding daily. Whether she did this winding herself, or asked a member of staff to do it for her, is open to question. She is also thought to have been a keen gardener – a type of begonia was named after her in 1907.

Her son Dan served in the army, but remained based at home. Her son Arthur was sent around the world with the navy, but married and eventually settled. Her daughter Joan did not marry, but lived in Oxfordshire for a time and also spent time in India and South Africa.

At the beginning of 1938 Muriel was taken ill and was not able to attend her usual public meetings and duties. Wishes were sent for her recovery to no effect, and she died in mid-February just shy of her 68th birthday. Many public institutions mourned her passing, with reports of her good work and benevolence given in the local newspapers.

When dealing with out-relief cases she was always just; with her own purse she was always generous.

Mr C.W.B. Oatley

No one more than the officers knew that vital work Lady Muriel did, and
the untiring energy she always put into everything she undertook. The
officers felt they had lost a true friend.

Mr Hussey
(both reported in the Wiltshire Times and Trowbridge Advertiser, *5.3.1938)*

In her will she left £26,500 to her husband. Her daughter Joan
died during the Second World War, and her son Dan died directly
afterwards. Muriel's husband Henry lived until 1953. In 1954, part of
their land was sold off to make a cattle market on Cocklebury Road.
Further probate was settled for Henry in 1957, when Chippenham
Council acquired the land and house. Muriel's house was divided up into
flats and is now in multiple ownership. An estate of houses was built on
some of the lands, with some streets named after the families that had
owned the house – and that's how Lady Coventry Road was named. The
rest of the land now forms a golf course and a public park.

References

Adams, C. (1982), *Ordinary Lives*, Virago Press
Bath Chronicle and Weekly Gazette, 7 April 1928, *New Wilts Magistrates*
Bristol Times and Mirror, 14 January 1892, *The Chippenham Ball*
Daniell, J.J. (1894), *The History of Chippenham*, R F Houlston
Devizes and Wiltshire Gazette, 15 September 1870, *Chippenham*
Devizes and Wilts Advertiser, 1 November 1917, *Chippenham*
England and Wales: Birth, Marriage and Death Records, held by Ancestry.co.uk
England and Wales: Christening Index 1530-1980, held by Ancestry.co.uk
Jefferies, S. (1987), *A Chippenham Collection*, Chippenham Civic Society
Liverpool Echo, 4 November 1933 *Keeping on terms with Father Time*
North Wilts Herald, 30 June 1911 *Chippenham Workhouse*
North Wilts Herald, 13 June 1913 *The Boy Scouts: Meeting at Chippenham*
The Salisbury Times, 16 November 1900 *Help the fighters*
UK 1851 census, held by Ancestry.co.uk
UK 1861 census, held by Ancestry.co.uk
UK 1871 census, held by Ancestry.co.uk
UK 1881 census, held by Ancestry.co.uk
UK 1891 census, held by Ancestry.co.uk
UK 1901 census, held by Ancestry.co.uk
UK 1911 census, held by Ancestry.co.uk
UK 1939 register, held by Ancestry.co.uk

Western Daily Press, 13 October 1904 *District news: Chippenham*
Western Daily Press, 6 May 1908, *Chippenham*
Western Daily Press, 22 February 1910, *Chippenham*
Western Daily Press, 16 December 1929 *For trial*
Wiltshire, England, Church of England Births and Baptisms 1813-1916, held by Ancestry.co.uk
Wiltshire Times and Trowbridge Advertiser, 7 November 1914, *Chippenham: The Belgian Refugees*
Wiltshire Times and Trowbridge Advertiser, 20 January 1923, *The Amateur Gilbert and Sullivan Operatic Society*
Wiltshire Times and Trowbridge Advertiser, 26 November 1932, *County Council By-election*
Wiltshire Times and Trowbridge Advertiser, 11 December 1937 *Home for the girls: Lady Coventry's Kind Act*
Wiltshire Times and Trowbridge Advertiser, 26 February 1938, *The Late Lady Muriel Coventry: A lifetime of public service*
Wiltshire Times and Trowbridge Advertiser, 5 March 1938, *The Late Lady Muriel Coventry. Guardians' Tributes*

Sarah Ann Tanner or Buckle or Hickling

S ARAH ANN TANNER, to use her original name, was widowed twice, ran various Chippenham pubs, and raised a clutch of children - not all of them her own. She would have been a well-known figure in the Chippenham of the later 19th and early 20th centuries, and – if women could have been at the time – would probably have been a good candidate for town mayor.

A plumber's daughter, Sarah was born in Chippenham in 1843 and grew up relatively comfortably in the 1840s and 50s in the rapidly-expanding market town. The establishment of the Great Western Railway in 1840 had meant that the settlement was now easily reachable from London, and businesses (and the population) were booming.

Her father's business grew big enough, probably due to the number of new houses needing plumbing, to support several employees and keep his daughters at home until they married rather than sending them out to work.

She was the youngest of at least seven siblings. However, while two of her elder sisters (Maria and Matilda) chose to remain at home until they wed, Sarah did not choose this route. By the age of 18 she and her eldest sister Mary, twelve years Sarah's senior, were running a seeds and food shop on Chippenham's High Street, which almost certainly saw good trade. They presumably lived above their shop, together. Her father had taken his three sons (John, William and George) into his business by 1861, so they could be considered a prominent local family.

At the age of 30, in the summer of 1861, her sister Mary married Jacob Buckland, a widowed yeoman farmer who later fixed pianos for a living, and presumably left Sarah to run the business herself. Her shop and its position on the High Street may have led Sarah to meet her own husband – Joseph Buckle, the widower landlord of The Bear Hotel, one of Chippenham's biggest hostelries on the town's market place – who she married at the age of 28, in the February of 1871.

This marriage gained her two step-children from her husband's previous marriage – Kate Buckle, aged 8, and Harry Buckle, aged 4 – and her husband had a stepson (William King) of his own from the first of his former wife's marriages. It also gained Sarah a pub, a business that kick started a career that lasted over 30 years.

Joseph Buckle had originally come to Chippenham from Gloucestershire, to work on the railway. At some point along the way, he'd met Mary Elizabeth Hobbs, a twice-widowed pub landlady who'd been in the trade since childhood as her father ran pubs on the town's Causeway. He married her in 1861, and they took on first the White Lion and then the Bear Hotel together, and she died in 1868. He then married Susanna Benger of the Bear Hotel in 1869, presumably one of his barmaids, but she died in July 1870. This also made him twice-widowed.

Although Joseph was named landlord, the 1871 census record has Sarah's occupation as a licenced victualler's wife at the Bear Hotel – indicating that she was fairly active in the day-to-day life of the establishment – but the enumerator concerned has crossed this description out, as it was considered invalid. The business was considered Joseph's, and as his wife Sarah was merely his property and helpmeet, rather than a businesswoman in her own right.

Sarah had her own daughter, Ada, a year or so after her marriage. She was heavily pregnant again with her son Joe in 1873 when her husband died suddenly, leaving her the business, his money, and their combined children. Her son was born a month after his father's death, and Sarah renewed the pub's licence in her name within another month.

She ran the pub with the help of her step-children and a couple of domestic servants for another three years until she married again. The marriage took place in 1877 at Chippenham's parish church, and was witnessed by her stepdaughter Kate.

Her second husband was Samuel Hickling, a former sergeant major from the 17th Lancers (who were famous for having taken part in the Charge of Light Brigade in the Crimean War, though there is no evidence to indicate he took part in that conflict). He originally came from Nottinghamshire, and in accordance with the law of the time he took over the hotel and pub licence – if the woman was married, her property became her husband's. In reality, Sarah probably continued running the pub as she had been, but she just wasn't given the credit.

The landlady and the barmaids were often the only women present in pubs at this time. They were mostly male domains – an occasional woman might eat there on a market day, if the pub served dinner – where men spent their leisure time away from home, and viewed as a respite from domestic matters. Sarah's job would have been much the same as any landlady or landlord today: serving ale and other alcoholic drinks, procuring the drinks from the brewery, washing glasses and keeping the establishment clean, entertaining the customers. There may well have been pub games on offer – bagatelle, shove-ha'penny, darts, cribbage, cards – and perhaps some singing late into the evening. The pub may also have provided accommodation, so there would also have been rooms to clean and prepare, and extra food to be cooked.

She and Samuel ran the pub together for another four years – with her stepdaughter Kate working as a barmaid – and had a daughter together in 1878. This was Gertrude Ethel Hickling, known to everyone as Ethel. Sarah and Samuel then gave up the business, and moved to a house on St Mary Street. It's unclear what they were surviving on – when their second daughter Elsie was baptised in Chippenham in 1885, Samuel's profession is given as a former soldier and a hotel business isn't mentioned – but it's possible that her inheritance from her first husband was enough to keep them comfortably.

However, this existence did not last. Samuel died in 1887, aged 40, leaving Sarah widowed for the second time. At this stage her stepchildren Kate and Harry were adults, but she had four dependent children – Joe aged 14 and daughters Ada aged 15, Ethel aged 9, and Elsie aged 2 – and no visible means of support.

Sarah therefore went back into the pub trade to provide for her family, based on the many years of experience she'd had at the hotel. She took on the Wine and Spirits Vaults in Chippenham's market place, just a stone's throw away from the Bear Hotel and ran that until 1892. This was located on the upper part of the market place, between the King's Head and the Duke of Cumberland, and close to the entrance to St Andrew's Church.

At this point business was clearly booming, despite the growth of the temperance movement and the location of a Temperance Hotel in nearby St Mary Street. For the next ten years Sarah took on The Three Cups, on the Market Place and The Shambles, and then ran the new successful Talbot Hotel from at some point before 1901, taking her business through to the early 20th century. She did not marry again, and therefore was able to keep the income and status her businesses generated. Her daughter Ada also worked alongside her in the business, serving in the bar and helping to run the hotel. Her other children and step-children would no doubt have helped out around their schooling, and she also kept her brother John on the premises as hotel manager.

William King, her first husband's stepson, went into the army. Her stepdaughter Kate Buckle became a matron at a hospital for the mentally ill in Gloucestershire, and does not appear to have married. Her stepson Harry Buckle married a woman named Kate Cummins and kept a grocery shop and pub in Bristol.

Of Sarah's own children, Ada Buckle married Walter John Hiscock, a linen draper who kept a shop in Chippenham Market Place, but also had dealings in other businesses - including a dairy. They had four children, but one died young. Walter was made town mayor in 1904, and served in that position again in 1916..

Ethel Hickling married a local veterinary surgeon, George Herbert Williams, and they lived at the now-demolished Clift House on Langley Road. Ethel became head cook at the Voluntary Aid Division Red Cross Hospital, which was housed in the Neeld Hall during the First World War.

Sarah's youngest daughter, Elsie Hickling, also went into nursing. She worked at the infirmary in Shoreditch, London. She married a soldier, Edward Miller, during the First World War.

In the early 1900s, when she was getting on in years, Sarah relinquished the pub trade and moved in with her unmarried son Joe Buckle as his housekeeper. He, and Ada's husband Walter Hiscock, ran a popular fishmongers and poultry shop on Chippenham's High Street in a timbered building that no longer exists, and it's likely that Sarah helped out with this business as she aged too. Joe also became the town's fire chief, and was a well-known local figure.

Having seen through the First World War and its hardships at Joe's shop, she died in Chippenham, aged 76, in the spring of 1920. Her son Joe eventually married four years after her demise.

References

Adams, C (1982), *Ordinary Lives*, Virago Press

Alder, R (2021), *Unity and Loyalty: The Story of Chippenham's Red Cross Hospital*, Chippenham Studies 5, Hobnob Press

Bristol Mercury - Thursday 17 August 1893, *Chippenham Flower Show*

Devizes and Wiltshire Gazette, Thursday 12 April 1866, *Notice*

Devizes and Wiltshire Gazette, Thursday 22 April 1869, *Births, marriages and deaths*

England and Wales: Birth, Marriage and Death Records, held by Ancestry.co.uk

Jefferies, S (1987), *A Chippenham Collection*, Chippenham Civic Society

North Wilts Herald, Saturday 1 March 1879, *Chippenham Times*

UK 1851 census, held by Ancestry.co.uk

UK 1861 census, held by Ancestry.co.uk

UK 1871 census, held by Ancestry.co.uk

UK 1881 census, held by Ancestry.co.uk

UK 1891 census, held by Ancestry.co.uk

UK 1901 census, held by Ancestry.co.uk

UK 1911 census, held by Ancestry.co.uk

UK 1939 register, held by Ancestry.co.uk

Wilts and Gloucestershire Standard, 9 January 1892, *Petty sessions*

Wiltshire Times and Trowbridge Advertiser, 28 April 1877, *Marriages*

May Ottley or Alexander

M AY OTTLEY WAS, in effect, a health and beauty influencer. But, in the late 19th and early 20th centuries, her sphere was in magazines and journals aimed at middle- and upper-class women with time on their hands for personal improvement, rather than carefully curated videos and hacks on the internet. Her advice and tips appeared in a range of publications at that time, but the only time she stepped out of that area her writing supposedly caused an embarrassing scandal in the Wiltshire village she resided, and the rumour is that she and her family were asked to leave on the back of it.

She didn't write under her actual birth name, however. She moonlighted as Dame Deborah Primrose, and for many years that name seems to have been synonymous with various products and treatments that she recommended and promoted. The original Deborah Primrose was a creation of playwright and novelist Oliver Goldsmith in the mid-1700s. His novel, *The Vicar of Wakefield: A Tale, Supposed to be written by Himself*, was published in 1766 and followed the life of the titular character Dr Charles Primrose and his wife Deborah. The Deborah Primrose created by Goldsmith was keen on clothes and beauty, and it may be that May found that this character resonated with her own interests.

The literary references also point to May having been well educated, particularly for a woman in this period. This appears to have been true. She was born May Alexander in 1872 in Hampstead, to Frederick Alexander – a bank clerk and later a banker – and his wife Janet née Baptie. She grew up initially in a villa next to Hampstead Heath, and then later in a smart newly-built town house a few streets further away.

She was the youngest of four children. Her two older brothers, Philip and Sidney, both attended Oxford University – with Philip matriculating at Hertford College and eventually becoming a school master, and Sidney climbing the academic ranks at first Trinity and then

Keble Colleges and winning an array of prizes. He eventually became a reverend, and a poet of great note, and was appointed a canon of Gloucester Cathedral in 1902.

May's older sister Janet received enough education to become a school teacher by 1891, when she married an eminent physiologist, and produced at least six children. In contrast, May seems to have taken her education further than her sister. She is later referred to, by biographers of Walter Pater, as having been a pupil of his sister Clara Pater. Walter Pater, an English essayist, art and literary critic and fiction writer, lived and worked in Oxford and was supported by his two sisters Clara and Hester. Clara, an expert in classical civilisations, was part of the Ladies Committee for Higher Education at Oxford, and became classics tutor at Somerville Hall for women on its establishment in 1879. She was then resident tutor of Somerville from 1885 until 1894. For May Alexander to have been her pupil, she almost certainly lived and was educated at Somerville. Lectures at Oxford were open to women from 1882 onwards, so in the period she attended she would have had access to tuition, even if she was unable to receive a degree – a situation that didn't change for women until 1920.

Somerville Hall was renamed Somerville College in 1894, which was also the year that Clara Pater retired and her brother Walter died. May's association with the Pater family continued though, as Clara Pater had become a personal friend.

The summer of 1894 was also when the first advice piece attributed to May, as Dame Deborah Primrose, is referenced as having been published in the weekly *Hearth and Home* journal. She was reported as recommending Aspinall's Neigeline, a preparation for the skin.

> It is excellent to apply for evening use, as it gives as soft clear look to the skin. The ingredients are perfectly harmless; you may accept my guarantee for this. It is so much better to get a really good thing of the kind, made by a man who has a reputation to sustain, than to bedaub your skin with all sorts of unknown compounds emanating from goodness knows where, and made of goodness knows what – generally cheap and nasty.

The fact that Dame Deborah Primrose is being quoted as an authority during this year may point to the idea that May was contributing articles to *Hearth and Home* earlier than 1894, but this reference – from an advert in *Globe* – is the first reference of its kind. It seems that May remained in Oxford, and supported herself for three years with various writing gigs for women's magazines and journals of the day – including *Myra's Journal of Dress and Fashion, World of Dress,* and *Gentlewoman.*

May married in 1897. Her husband was Robert Lawrence Ottley, an academic theology star at Oxford who was Hertford Scholar in 1876, Craven Scholar in 1879, tutor at Christ Church College in 1881, Principal of Cuddesdon Theological College in 1886, Divinity Dean at Magdalen College in 1890, and in 1893 – as a reverend – was appointed principal librarian of the Pusey House. The Pusey House was, and remains today, a space for sacred learning and worship.

Robert's formative education, however, derived from his older sister Alice Ottley – who, after the death of her vicar father took in paying pupils and became a well-respected name in 19th century girls' education. In 1883 she had become head teacher of Worcester High School for Girls, having been recommended to a local canon, and remained in post until retiring in 1912. The school was named the Alice Ottley School in her honour in 1914.

Therefore, the marriage must have seemed advantageous for May, but she was also marrying someone who absolutely supported the importance of education for women. Straight after the marriage, Robert accepted the Magdalen College living of the vicarage of Winterbourne Bassett in Wiltshire. May went with him, and settled into married life in the parish. Their first child, daughter Constance Mary, was born in 1898 at May's family home in Hampstead, but baptised by her father at the church in Winterbourne Bassett.

May was still writing for various women's journals on health and beauty matters alongside her new motherhood. The autumn edition of *Hearth and Home* for 1898 included her work (alongside Mrs Dorothy Lane on Dress, Mrs Talbot Coke on Home Advice, and Mrs Fitzmaurice on Art of the Needle), so there was no question of her giving up work because she had had a baby.

A second daughter, Agnes May, followed in 1899 and then a third – Lucy Janet but always known as Janet – in 1901, both while the family were living at Winterbourne Bassett. Her vicarage household was aided by a nursemaid, a housemaid and a cook, so she had more time than many other women of that period to pursue interests outside the home. An edition of *Gentlewoman* from November 1902 has her recommending

a quality hair stain – Saonetto – to correspondents, having tried out
scores of them. Apparently *'if the instructions are carefully carried out,
the hair can be washed as usual every fourth week, and the stain will remain
good for several months. It never comes off on hat linings or pillows.'* Washing
hair once a month may seem disgusting today, but this advice was
very common in Edwardian times when most people would only take
a bath once a week. May's advice was still being quoted in Saonetto
adverts until the early 1920s. She also advised against corsets in *Hearth
and Home*, suggesting them unnecessary, an idea remarked upon by a
columnist from the *Yorkshire Gazette* in 1903. The writer suggested that,
contrary to Dame Deborah Primrose's opinion, properly made corsets
both supported the figure and enhanced female beauty.

However, in 1904, May turned her pen away from health and
beauty and wrote a book on an entirely different subject – the villagers
that surrounded her in Winterbourne Bassett. Entitled *A Modern Bœotia*,
she again wrote under her *nom de plume* Deborah Primrose – but this may
have also been to hide her true identity rather than promote her other
work as the contents of the book could be described as highly critical of
the village at best and at worst possibly inflammatory and potentially
insulting. Described in adverts as *'As entertaining as a novel'*, the book was
published by Methuen in April 1904.

The title of the book did not set things up well for May's view of
the rural village she lived in. Bœotia was a rural region of ancient Greece
where cultured Athenians considered the people dull, stupid, simple and
uncultured. May, in linking the two, was showing her deep educational
knowledge but also casting considerable aspersions on the people of the
village in which she lived.

Nicknaming Winterbourne Bassett 'Snorum End' and describing
it as a backwater, May's opus looked at different characters, manners,
customs and facets of society within the village social structure from the
perspective of Rector Dr Christopher Primrose and his wife Deborah,
drawing a loose comparison with Goldsmith's earlier novel. She sets the
scene at the beginning of Chapter Two, *The Bœotians*:

> We came to Snorum End totally unprepared for the type of humanity
> with which we found it was our lot to deal. Our ideas of country people
> had been garnered partly from an entirely superficial acquaintance,
> partly, with the assistance of Crabbe and Wordsworth, and 'The Vicar of
> Wakefield' from our own facile, poetic imaginations.

With the aid of these illusive guides, we had painted in anticipation the picture of our village flock. They were affectionate, guileless people, easy to please, easy to love, easy to guide. The children were obedient, respectful, teachable, modest; their parents were plain, simple-hearted, simple-mannered folk.

Our hopes were destined to receive a somewhat rough shock, and we look at our people now with unidealistic gaze. Romance is dead within us, for we see them as they are.

A review in the *Salisbury and Winchester Journal*, from June that year, seems to have pinpointed roughly where May was writing from:

From the dialect and the descriptions of the landscape we should conjecture that the village is situated somewhere in Wiltshire, but it is not easy to guess in which part of the county it may be. There are hints given here and there which point to North Wilts, but these apparent clues may have been inserted with the intention of misleading the reader, for it is evident all through the book that 'Deborah Primrose' is not adverse to making quiet fun of people.

What for reviewers may have seemed making quiet fun, others may have found more difficult had they known their doings were being recorded. May's pen was particularly acerbic around village characters that she'd found in Winterbourne Bassett. For example, in the book she described the actions of the gravedigging sexton thus:

Our worthy sexton, in his work-a-day smock, but with professionally solemn face, has just been to announce the 'inkwidge' [*inquest, pronounced in a Wiltshire manner*] held to-day, in an adjacent parish, on an old woman whose main fault appeared to be that she lived too long and took an uncommon time dying.

When she fell ill, she was left for three weeks in bed in a cold, draughty room without a fire-place, and surrendered to the tender mercies of a grandchild of ten, and of a husband whose solicitude seems to have reached the point of administering an occasional 'cup o'tea' and of calling in the neighbours to 'take a look at she'. They looked, and advised medical aid, but the doctor was not sent for, and the result was what might have been expected. The woman died. 'And,' said old Robert, 'we brought in a verdick o'death from a national cause ma'am. Ashmia,

we told the crowner. 'Er wur a main stout 'ooman, main stout 'er wur,
and it hurted my feeldiu's it did, to look at she, lyin' so stout and so stiff.
You see ma'am,' this with a sudden change of voice and a knowing wink,
'we 'ad best say the wurred, and the crowner could ha' been down on he
terr'ble; but we looked at it this way. It could ha' done no good to she, and
it could have only done bad to he, so we said what we said. But we all had
to kiss the Book, ma'am, yes we all did have to kiss he.

It needed a very slight stretch of imagination to see the twelve good
men and true, ignorant as children of all except 'ship' and ''osses' and
'cabbages' overwhelmed with the sense of their sudden importance,
anxious to do their duty by the dead, but more anxious not to offend
the living; bribed, may be, by the promise of a 'pot o'beer' not to say
too much. So they 'said what they said', and came home on the whole
content, yet haunted by a lurking terror occasioned by the kissing of the
'Book'.

There are tales of other parishioners, from a woman eventually
charged with child neglect because her baby was 'black, and covered
with sores and worse than sores, and it was entirely naked', to another
who when cleaning made sure to wash all her china dog ornaments'
faces as if they were children. Another, a mother of eleven, is described
as having regularly fallen out with the auspices of both the church and
the non-conformist chapel, so that half her brood were baptised at each
institution and one was christened in a pudding basin.

Chronically ill Mrs Simpson is painted as never satisfied with
any comfort that May could bring her in her visiting role as vicar's wife,
complaining about every attempt to feed her foods that could bring her
to better health. And Mrs Jones, busy with baking and seven children,
is given as not intelligent enough to understand the difference between
ointment and medicine, and would rather give her oral-thrush-stricken
baby a folk cure.

There is old Mr Stannard, who may be any age between seventy-five and
ninety, toddling along, according to his afternoon custom, to the inn.
He has in days gone by, been a soldier and fought in the 'Muttony' and a
certain pathetic interest thereby attaches itself to the old childish face,
with its bleared eyes and towzled hair.

He always looks uncared for and unwashed, and it is very difficult to
catch the sense of his thick, muddled words. To-day, however, a feeble

smile lights up his poor foolish face, for news has just arrived of Lord
Roberts' entry into Pretoria.

'Well'm' with a pull at his tangled forelock, 'an' Oi 'ears tell as 'ow
they've token the king o' that there pleace, Vittoriey, an't it called? An' Oi
says 'Gawd save the Quane' and Oi wants to drenk 'er 'elth and 'struction
to all iminies.'

Throughout the book though, there is a sense that May was merely
enduring the life she was living but did not enjoy it or feel as if it was her
purpose – despite the fact that that both she and her husband must have
shared a deep Christian faith to have been placed in the Winterbourne
Bassett living in the first place. Her tone seems to place her rather above
the concerns of the village instead of part of them.

From the more glaring vices they are on the whole conspicuously free,
but sometimes one feels one could bear them to be drunkards or even
worse, if only they would love. But these passionate, empty natures are so
difficult of access, so far remote from all that lends grace and beauty and
attractiveness to human character, that I often feel inclined to sit down
in profound pessimism.

Reviews of *A Modern Bœotia* were generally positive. The *Sheffield
Daily Telegraph*, on 11 May 1904, said that 'The quaintness of the country
permeates the whole book and it will be found thoroughly readable by
town and country alike.' *St James' Gazette* review of 21 July 1904 says:
'so keen is the insight, so simple yet graphic the style of the parson's
wife who plays the part of chroniciler (sic), that the small beer has been
converted into a draught of still, clear, white wine of full flavour and
fine bouquet.' The *Salisbury and Winchester Journal*, on 28 May 1904,
described the work as

a charming and brilliant book, and we can cordially recommend it to
our readers. If these very clever and interesting sketches are received by
the public with the favour they deserve, it is to be hoped that they will
be followed by other works from the same pen. With her fine faculty of
observation, her admirable talent for depicting character, her graceful
style and her qualities as a descriptive writer, 'Deborah Primrose' ought
to have it in her power to achieve considerable success as a novelist.

The story goes that after this book was published, the parishioners of Winterbourne Bassett were deeply offended and that May's husband Robert was quietly removed from the living at the village and posted elsewhere. However, in August 1903, a full nine months before the book was published, Robert had been made a canon of Christ Church, Oxford, and Regius Professor of Pastoral Theology, so the Ottley family had vacated the living at Winterbourne Bassett and returned to Oxford.

This may have given May the impetus to publish her notes from the parish, feeling that she could now do so without detection. But it seems that someone, somewhere, had some idea of the authorship – or the story of the removal of Robert on its publication would not have arisen. And it may be that the backlash this caused meant that May did not feel that the predicted success as a novelist suggested by reviewers was for her, as she never seems to have published anything in this ilk again.

Back in the academic world of Oxford, May both had a fourth daughter – Ursula Margaret – and with Heineman published a different type of book in 1905. This work, *Beauty of figure: how to acquire and retain it by means of easy and practical home exercises*, was far more in keeping with her previous writing on health and beauty matters, and indeed built upon that reputation. May expounded on her beliefs in the introduction:

Beauty of figure or form, being the expression of perfect health and

proper proportion, has been an idea at which the thinking majority of
the human race has aimed in all time, and those who try to show us that
'physical culture,' as we understand the phrase, is some cult of to-day and
perchance of to-morrow, exhibit a very slight knowledge of the history of
their forerunners on this little round earth.

The book was more of an exercise manual, looking at sequences
for different body parts that could be achieved in the home and could
improve the person both physically and mentally – in common with
much Edwardian societal rhetoric. Most of the exercises were advocated
to be done in the company of other women, out of the gaze of the
menfolk.

Talking of finding a suitable time for this exercise reminds me of
a practical illustration of the value of skipping in the promotion
of beauty in the figure. A lady of my acquaintance, obliged by the
sedentary nature of her work to sit indoors many hours each day, found
herself becoming much too stout for comfort or elegance, and a kind
and candid friend advised her to try a quarter of an hour's skipping
once a day. Living in a neighbourhood where the barrel-organ is still
appreciated, she, taking the advice in the kindly way it was meant, and
the earnest way in which she does everything, so arranged her work
that when the daily organ came to her end of the street she could take
her skipping rope into her paved back-yard and she soon learned to skip
in regular measure to the rhythmic sounds. She has encouraged her
two daughters to join her in this exercise, and all are now slim, upright,
healthy and buoyant.

There was an extra chapter on Anglo-Swedish exercises – these
being particularly popular in school physical training drills at the time
– which looked at working several muscle groups at once. And a chapter
on special exercises for stout women, this physical trait being seen as
particularly undesirable. May signed off this book with another literary
quote,

And my last word is to remind all women that the poet Thomson, in the
year 1700, said:
    Health is the vital principle of bliss.
    And exercise of health.

and a raft of adverts for products that she recommended – *Hearth and Home* journal, hair stain, face creams, wrinkle smoothers, corsets and even a hotel.

This book appears to have been May's last, though her magazine writing and advice career continued. Her recommendations are regularly quoted in newspaper advertisements, from her writing in *Woman*, *Gentlewoman*, and the erstwhile *Hearth and Home* – from a pamphlet on care of teeth to an exaltation of velveteen fabric seized upon by the *Guardian*.

A 1905 edition of *Woman* had Dame Deborah Primrose holding forth on *The Woman Beautiful*, while that October's edition of *Gentlewoman* had May's full support of the beauty methods of high-end salon owner Mrs Eleanor Adair. With bases in London, Paris and New York, Mrs Adair's most famous product was her patented Ganesh chin and forehead straps – patches worn over these areas at night to reduce wrinkles and firm skin – which were embedded with mysticism from the East from their inventor's trip to the Vale of Kashmir. The article finds May in full beauty influencer mode:

> Of this class of energetic women who fully realise the responsibility of undertaking the culture and preservation of beauty of other women is Mrs Adair, of 90 New Bond Street, London, W., a gentlewoman of handsome and distinguished presence who has had exceptional opportunities for travel and for medical training and specialising.
>
> In a distant land she discovered the value of preserving the contour of the face by upholding the chin during the hours when the jaws and the muscles of the cheeks involuntarily relax, just as do the rest of the muscles of our bodies, when we sleep.
>
> The support so perfectly given by the 'Ganesh Chin Strap' she invented as the outcome of this discover, is sufficient to preserve the youthful outlines of the face indefinitely if the wearing of it is commenced early enough, while this silken thing is strong enough to send away an embarrassing 'double-chin' if regularly worn at night for a reasonable period.

She also recommended a product called 'Dr Horn's Pasta Reducer' in an edition of *Woman* at some point before 1907 – as that publication shut down that year. This was designed to make the bust firm and reduce its size and flaccidity. It was probably some type of paste or concoction, rather than a contraption like the Ganesh straps.

Away from her writing, May continued to live in Oxford with her family, and had her fifth and final daughter – Dorothea Mary – there in the autumn of 1908. She continued to enjoy a friendship with Clara Pater, who died in 1910, and her sister Hester Pater who survived her.

Just after Christmas in 1910 it was wrongly reported that her husband Robert had died. In fact, it had been his brother – Reverend Edward Bickersteth Ottley, a canon of Rochester Cathedral – who had passed on, and this was reported in *Clifton Society*. However, no less than 11 newspapers confused Edward with Robert and it was widely reported that Robert, described as a distinguished Oxford cleric and author, had died at Seaforth. Robert was in fact alive and well, but no retraction ever seems to have been printed.

Indeed, May can be found with Robert and all their daughters in Teignmouth the following spring on the 1911 census. Robert does not appear to have taken up another parish living, so this is likely to have been a seaside holiday from Oxford rather than their usual place of residence. They had taken two servants with them to help with the children.

As the next decade rumbled on, so did May's printed health and beauty advice. Though this was at a reduced rate than before. She's reported as recommending Mrs Kendrick's Herb Tea to help with Obesity in *Hearth and Home* in 1912, a parting postiche – a false hairpiece – in *The Queen* in 1914, and antiseptic foot powder in *Hearth and Home* in 1918. Her husband was also publishing religious books at this time. Since they had no sons, they did not send family off to war in 1914 like many families at that time, but many of their daughters fostered an interest in medicine so may have been involved in the volunteer medical efforts at home.

May's recommendations for various beauty products continue to appear in newspaper adverts until around 1920, some of them being quoted 15-20 years after her advice was first published. On the 1921 census, where the family were resident at Christ Church College in Oxford, in accommodation that came with her husband's job, May referred to herself as a teacher. This gives an idea of what had replaced her focus as her influencer role in magazines had waned. Exactly what she was teaching and where isn't clear from the record, but given her background it is likely to have been literature or classics at some

institution in Oxford. All five daughters are still at home, though eldest
Constance is given as a medical student at London Hospital, and second
daughter Agnes is a history student at Oxford University. The family
belief in educating women well was continuing into this new generation,
and indeed Agnes was honourably mentioned for the Oxford Chancellor's
prize for best English essay in 1922.

May's old friend Hester Pater, sister of Walter and Clara, died in
August 1922. May and her husband Robert were appointed her probate
executors, and as a result May inherited a large portion of Walter Pater's
books, papers and remaining estate. In the years since Clara's death,
Hester and the Ottleys had occasionally attempted to publish some
of Walter's remaining manuscripts, but this had not come to fruition.
However, this bequest put these works in the hands of May and Robert.
And as part of Pater's remaining heirs, the possession of his estate meant
that May and Robert received 50 per cent of the profits of his Macmillan-
published books that were sold in London. This continued until 1925.

Working together, Robert and May were keen on two unpublished
Pater manuscripts – *Imaginary Portraits. An English Poet*; Johnson's *Lives
of the Poets* – and wrote to Macmillan in 1924 to ask if they'd consider
publishing them in future editions. The response was negative. Later,
May managed to persuade *The Fortnightly Review* journal to publish *An
English Poet* in 1931, and her headnote mentions that she had done some
limited editing of Pater's text to ready it for print.

Robert died at their Christ Church home in early February
1933, aged 77. He still held the Regius Professor title at his death, and
newspapers noted him as a theological author of some gravitas. His
previous supposed death reports are not mentioned in his actual death
notices. His death meant that May had to leave their Christ Church
lodgings, as his role and accommodation went to Reverend Kenneth
Escott Kirk by the end of that March.

Eldest daughter Constance was at this time a well-respected
surgeon attached to a women's hospital at Hove on the south Sussex
coast, and May and three of her daughters are reported by a later-
published *The Pater Society Newsletter* to have moved down there to live
with her. May also was now the sole remaining heir of Walter Pater's
estate, and her share of his royalties was due to run until 1944.

May died at their Wilbury Road home in Hove on 3 August
1939, aged 66. She was buried in Hove Cemetery, and she left all her
property – including the Pater legacy – to eldest daughter Constance.

The only one of May's daughters to marry, her youngest Dorothea, had
made her match the previous spring and gone off to London to live
with her new husband. Third daughter Janet had gone into nursing,
and was matron at the voluntary hospital in Cardiff during the Second
World War. Fourth daughter Ursula was also serving on the nursing
staff at that hospital. Second daughter Agnes held the principal of St
Katherine's teacher training college on White Hart Lane in London for
many years. Constance had a long career as a surgeon, and wrote some
journal articles in the early 1950s discussing the links between cigarette
smoking and lung cancer, and when she died in 1981 she passed the
Pater legacy to her remaining sisters.

References

Atherstone News and Herald, 30 December 1910, *Canon Robert Lawrence Ottley*
Bath Chronicle and Weekly Gazette, 4 September 1879, *University, Educational
    &c*
The Belfast Newsletter, 7 December 1892, *Birth, Marriage and Death Notices*
Bennett, J (2023), *Cosmetics and skin: Eleanor Adair*, at https://
    cosmeticsandskin.com/companies/adair.php (accessed 1/1/2024)
Chelmsford Chronicle, 4 May 1906, *Gates of Pearl*
Cheshire Observer, 24th June 1905, *Beauty*
Clifton Society, 22 December 1910, *The Rev. Edward Bickersteth Ottley*
England and Wales: Birth, Marriage and Death Records, held by Ancestry.co.uk
England and Wales: Christening Index 1530-1980, held by Ancestry.co.uk
Foster, J. (1893), *Oxford Men and Their Colleges, 1880-1892, including
    matriculation register*, Stephen Austin and Sons
Gentlewoman, 29 November 1902, *Extract from a letter to a correspondent to
    Dame Deborah Primrose*
Gentlewoman, 14 October 1905, *Trustworthy methods of beauty culture – Mrs
    Adair's*
Gentlewoman, 22 May 1909, *Reliable beauty books*
Gentlewoman, 21 August 1909, *True economy in beauty culture*
Globe, 12 July 1894, *Apinall's Neigeline.*
Globe, 2 April 1904, *The same firm publish shortly...*
Gloucester Citizen, 2 February 1933, *Dr Robert Ottley: Noted Theological Author
    Dead*
Goldsmith, O. (1766) *The Vicar of Wakefield: A Tale, Supposed to be written by
    Himself*, R. Collins
The Guardian from London, 7 November 1906, *Velveteens, Velveteens*
Inman, B.A. (1983) Note: Tracing the Pater Legacy in The Pater Society
    Newsletter, International Walter Pater Society, University of Arizona
Inman, B. A. (1995) *Tracing the Pater Legacy, Part II: Posthumous Sales,*

Manuscripts and Copyrights, in The Pater Newsletter, International Walter Pater Society, University of Arizona

Inman, B.A (1998) *May Ottley's Other Persona*, in The Pater Newsletter, International Walter Pater Society, University of Arizona

Kirkintilloch Herald, 19 June 1918, *Beauty, health and comfort*

London Evening Standard, 12 October 1897, *The Bampton Lectures for 1897*

London Evening Standard, 19 February 1915, *New books*

Medical Women's Federation Quarterly/Journal Summer 1981. *Obituary: Ottley, Constance Mary. Born, 1898; died, 1981.*

Myra's Journal of Dress and Fashion, 1 July 1908, *Woman. Summer double number.*

Myra's Journal of Dress and Fashion, 1 November 1908, *The Autumn fashion number*

Myra's Journal of Dress and Fashion, 1 November 1908, *The woman beautiful in Scotland*

Myra's Journal of Dress and Fashion, 1 August 1909, *Stout People*

Myra's Journal of Dress and Fashion, 1 January 1910, *Grand Christmas Competition*

North Down Herald and County Down Independent, 13 September 1912, *Obesity. The safe, simple, sure remedy*

Northern Whig, 30 March 1933, *The King has Approved the appointment...*

Oxfordshire Blue Plaques Board (2023) *Oxfordshire Blue Plaques Scheme*, at https://www.oxonblueplaques.org.uk/plaques/pater.html (accessed 1/1/2024)

Oxford Chronicle and Reading Gazette, 28 August 1903, *Installation of Canon Ottley*

Oxford Chronicle and Reading Gazette, 9 June 1922, *Chancellor's prize for English Essay*

Pickard-Cambridge, A. W. (1904) *A Modern Bœotia,* The Economic review, 1891-1914 ; London, Vol. 14, Iss. 4, (Oct 1904): 509-510.

Primrose, D. (1904) *A Modern Bœotia*, Methuen

Primrose, D (1905) *Beauty of figure: how to acquire and retain it by means of easy and practical home exercises*, Heineman

The Queen, 8 October 1898, *The autumn fashion number of Hearth and Home.*

The Queen, 23 November 1907, *Hygiene at Miss Johnson*

The Queen, 19 December 1908, *Trustworthy methods of beauty culture*

The Queen, 6 August 1910, *The removal of crow's feet*

The Queen, 4 April 1914, *Hemple's Patent Parting Postiche*

Roscommon Messenger, 30 September 1905, *'Woman' as a journal of information*

Salisbury and Winchester Journal, 27 May 1893, *Ecclesiastical*

Salisbury and Winchester Journal, 28 May 1904, *Reviews: A Modern Bœotia*

Somerville, University of Oxford, (2023) *From hall to college*, at https://www.some.ox.ac.uk/about/a-brief-history-of-somerville/from-hall-to-college/ (accessed 1/1/2024)

Sunderland Daily Echo and Shipping Gazette, 2 February 1933, *Dr Ottley Dead*

Sheffield Daily Telegraph, 11 May 1904, *Entertaining village pictures*

St James's Gazette, Thursday 21 July 1904, *There is something entirely fresh...*
UK census collection, held by Ancestry.co.uk
Wells Journal, 25 November 1897, *Church news*
Westminster Gazette, 29 April 1904, *Methuen's Popular Novels*
Wiltshire, England, Church of England Deaths and Burials, 1813-1922, held by Ancestry.co.uk
Yorkshire Gazette, 26 September 1903, *In defence of corsets*
Yorkshire Post and Leeds Intelligencer, 3 February 1933, *Canon Ottley: Oxford Professor of Theology*

Index

This is primarily an index of people and places, including streets and some buildings within towns. A few subjects and themes have also been indexed. Entries for women who are the subjects of biographies are in **bold**.

About the author ~~

LUCY WHITFIELD is a hands-on creative history practitioner and research obsessive.

People and their stories are at the heart of everything that she does, whether that be introducing adults to their ordinary extraordinary female ancestors, educating school children about skills their forebears would have possessed, demonstrating medieval headdresses and hand spinning at a family open day, or teaching workshops on the sailor's hornpipe at a folk festival.

She is the founder of *The Women Who Made Me* project, which researches and profiles ordinary extraordinary women across history and aims to inspire people to re-evaluate and reconnect with their female relatives, and her discoveries have been broadcast on BBC radio and exhibited in museums. She regularly talks to groups about her work, and displays at museums and history centres.

Lucy always says that she collects interesting women, both personally and professionally, and is usually knee deep in researching her latest discovery. She also has an archaeology degree, used to be a journalist, and once made a crop circle.

But that's another story...

www.lucywhitfieldhistorian.co.uk

Milton Keynes UK
Ingram Content Group UK Ltd.
UKHW021035170524
442867UK00006B/442